CW01080441

Q&A

Questions and Answers

The Marine Aquarium

Q&A

Questions and Answers

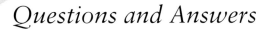

The Marine Aquarium

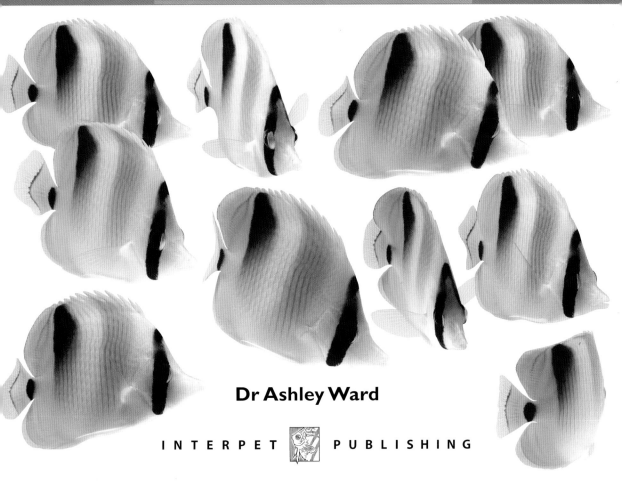

Dr Ashley Ward

INTERPET PUBLISHING

ISBN 978-1-84286-168-4

This reprint 2009

Credits

Created and compiled:
Ideas into Print, Claydon,
Suffolk IP6 0AB, England.

Design and prepress:
Stuart Watkinson, Ayelands,
Longfield, Kent DA3 8JW, England.

Computer graphics:
Stuart Watkinson

Production management:
Consortium, Poslingford, Suffolk
CO10 8RA, England

Printed and bound in China

Author

Dr Ashley Ward, BSc is a Research Fellow in the School of Biology at the University of Sydney, Australia. He is a fish biologist, conducting research into the behaviour of marine fishes. During his career, he has looked at a wide range of different aspects of fish behaviour, including fish intelligence, feeding and shoaling behaviour and the breeding behaviour of cichlids. As well as studying fish in the aquarium, Dr Ward takes every opportunity to get out into the wild to study fish in their natural environment.

Below: Such a mouth leaves little doubt that this grouper is a predator!

Q&A

The Marine Aquarium

Contents

The Marine Aquarium

Introduction

Tropical marine fish and invertebrates are amongst the most dazzlingly colourful animals on the planet, leading to their description by many as 'living jewels'. Yet as aquarists and divers alike have often realised, their amazing behaviour patterns and lifestyles perhaps even exceed the drama of their appearance. Watching them can often provoke questions such as 'Why are they behaving like this?' or 'How does it do that?' Understanding the 'hows' and the 'whys' of their behaviour adds a new dimension to the hobby. In this book, I will take a comprehensive look at the fascinating elements of fish and invertebrate behaviour on coral reefs around the world.

Left: *Lively chromis are excellent reef aquarium fish.*

7

Chapter 1
The coral reef

The clear, warm waters of the tropics are home to perhaps the most dramatic environment on earth – the coral reef. Here we find the most breathtaking groups of animals, both in terms of their incredible colours and sheer numbers.

The reefs themselves are constructed by countless coral polyps – relatives of anemones and jellyfish. Each polyp lives as a free-swimming larva before abandoning the water column and settling on the reef. When it does so, the polyp forms its own protective, cuplike, calcium skeleton around itself, where it can retreat if threatened. Once settled, the polyp begins to reproduce asexually, growing and expanding to form a colony of thousands, or even millions, of connected clones until it reaches sexual maturity (see page 182-183).

Q: *How do single polyps build into a reef?*

A: In hard, reef-building corals, each generation of polyps builds upon the last, so that the reef itself has a coating of living polyps on a core of the dead limestone skeletons of their forebears. This layer-upon-layer building can, over time, be sufficient to form colossal geological structures, such as Australia's Great Barrier Reef. This tendency of tiny polyps to construct an entire habitat, providing food and shelter to a whole host of other animals, is the reason that reefs are so amazingly populous and diverse. Soft corals also settle as polyps on surfaces, but do not construct the same kind of limestone skeletons. Instead, their skeleton is reduced to supporting rods throughout their tissue. Despite this, soft corals can still produce incredible and dazzling structures, often branched and coated in brilliantly coloured polyps.

Q: *What conditions do reef-building corals require to grow?*

A: The warm waters of the world's tropics are not the only places where corals can grow, but they are the home of the reef-building corals. In order to flourish, these corals require warmth and bright

Left: Stony coral polyps emerge from their limestone stronghold to feed on passing plankton. Huge reef structures are built by generations of coral polyps.

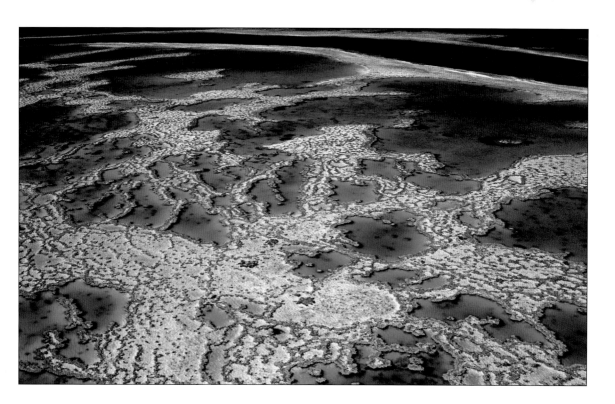

Above: The Great Barrier Reef is one of the wonders of the world – 2000km long and rising 200m from the sea bed in places.

light. This usually means ocean temperatures of 20-28°C and shallow waters, where the sunlight can penetrate to feed the symbiotic algae that live in the coral's tissue. For this same reason, the coral needs clear water – suspended matter scatters light – so healthy reefs are seldom found near estuaries or, nowadays, too near industrial cities. Reefs also benefit from

wave action and water currents, which not only deliver food and nutrients to the polyps, but also prevent excessive sedimentation on the reef. Perhaps because of the fact that they live in comparatively nutrient-poor waters, corals have evolved to be highly efficient. Not only do they harness the sun's energy, they can take calcium to construct their skeletons directly from the water, and their symbiotic algae can recycle animal wastes in order to photosynthesise. In doing so, the algae produce the sugars needed both by themselves and the coral.

Q: *Where in the world are coral reefs found?*

A: Coral reefs are found in the belt encircling the globe known as the tropics. The seas found here are characterised by stable temperature and light conditions, as well as bright sunshine. Reefs occur in the Caribbean, the Red Sea and across the Indo-Pacific. They can also be found beyond the tropics, for example in southern Japan, where currents carry warm waters to these shores, creating the necessary conditions for reef growth.

Coral reef ecology

Coral reefs are home to an incredibly diverse range of organisms, in many cases living at densities that far exceed those found in other aquatic habitats. This is despite the fact that, in most cases, corals live in waters with low levels of nutrients. The total number of fish species that either live on the coral reefs, or are associated with them at some point during their lives, is estimated at between 6,000 and 8,000. Put another way, that is well over one third of all the known fish species in the world in a habitat that occupies less than 1% of the world's seas.

Q: Apart from fish, what other types of animal are found on coral reefs?

A: Coral reefs are also home to a bewildering number of invertebrate species, including crustaceans (such as shrimps, lobsters and crabs), echinoderms (starfish and sea urchins, for example), sponges, worms, molluscs and sea squirts, to name but a few. There are even thousands of species of coral itself. Of the 34 different animal phyla on Earth (each phylum is a taxonomically distinct group), 32 occur on coral reefs. When compared with rainforests, where nine, or at the most 10, can be found, it is easy to see why biologists consider coral reefs to be unique.

Q: Why are coral reefs so diverse?

A: This is one of the biggest questions in ecology and several answers have been proposed.

The diversity of reefs

Different types of coral tend to flourish in particular zones: some – usually stony corals – can survive the pounding of the waves and gain the richest food supply, while softer corals can only survive in the shelter of the inner lagoon.

A fringing reef thrives at the shore, protected by the outer reef.

Fringing reefs also develop in the calm waters of the lagoon.

Platform reefs can form long stretches of calm, shallow water.

Smaller reefs inside the lagoon may eventually develop into platforms.

Barrier reefs separate the open sea from the lagoon.

A typical fringing reef

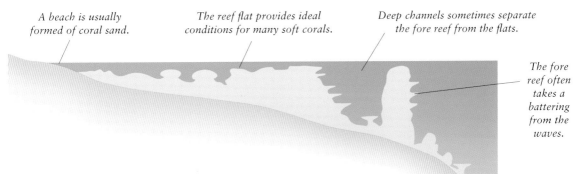

A beach is usually formed of coral sand.

The reef flat provides ideal conditions for many soft corals.

Deep channels sometimes separate the fore reef from the flats.

The fore reef often takes a battering from the waves.

One popular current theory holds that the very high levels of predation experienced by all reef animals reduces the probability of any species becoming dominant on the reef through its ability to out-compete others. But although it is difficult to say exactly what their relative importance is, it seems very likely that high productivity, high competition and high predation have all played a significant role in the evolution of so many different species on coral reefs. Another facet of reef communities is that they are actually quite robust. Amongst the millions of individuals representing thousands of species found on the average reef, large population cycles and fluctuations happen year after year, yet the community remains working and intact. One reason for this is that if a species has a

bad year – caused, for example, by poor recruitment of juveniles to the reef following their larval drifting stage, or by relentless competition or predation – there is always another species available to fulfil its ecological role. So if one grazing herbivore becomes locally rare, there are plenty of others ready to step in.

Q: *What different habitats can be found in the tropical marine ecosystem?*

A: Many coastal reefs have very distinct zones – the sheltered lagoon is protected from the battering of the waves and here seagrass meadows form in the warm shallow waters. Delicate corals are better able to grow on the lagoon side of the reef, again because of the protection from the waves. Heading in towards

the shore from the fore reef, the shallow reef flats are bathed in sunshine. Here, numerous algae species use the sun to photosynthesise and are in turn grazed by fish and invertebrates. Sometimes this reef flat stretches for hundreds of metres and can be exposed at low tide. Occasionally, there may be breaks and channels in the reef, allowing direct communication between the lagoon and the open sea. These areas are often associated with strong water currents and can be a favourite haunt of filter-feeders and planktivorous fish. The seaward face of the fore reef descends from the crest near the ocean surface down to the sea floor. The upper parts of the reef face are well supplied with nutrients and food, delivered by the ocean currents, but are also exposed to the waves. Only the toughest corals can survive here.

Living on the reef

Fish are one of the most successful groups of animals on the planet. There are over 20,000 species of fish, occupying every imaginable habitat. In each case, evolution has shaped both their appearance and their senses over countless generations and millions of years, resulting in the most effective adaptations to fit the conditions in which they live.

Q: *How are fish adapted for living on coral reefs?*

A: Although thousands of fish species live on coral reefs, most conform broadly to a handful of body plans. Perhaps the most common shape for reef fishes is a deep, laterally compressed body, as seen in butterflyfishes, damselfishes and angelfishes. The deep body is perfect for intricate manoeuvring in the water column above the reef, where the fish pick at their invertebrate prey or graze on algae with specialised mouthparts. Their wafer-thin profile also allows them to take refuge in the narrowest gaps and fissures in the reef. The long and slender bodies of hunters, such

as moray eels and trumpetfish, allow them access to the heart of the labyrinth of the reef – ideal when hunting sheltering fish and invertebrates. Other species, including blennies, gobies and many wrasse, live close to the substrate or hug the reef as they swim and feed on benthic (bottom-living) invertebrates. Their long, thin bodies enable them to seek shelter in the reef.

Q: *Which senses do coral reef fish use most?*

A: The waters of coral reefs are extremely clear and well lit by the equatorial sun. In addition, most reef fish live close to the surface. Under these conditions, vision is extremely important and this is reflected in the large eyes common to many of these fish. The brilliant colours, including vivid yellows and electric blues, and the dramatic patterns seen in many reef fishes are also features of brightly lit environments. Fish send bold visual signals to one another. However, to back up their vision, they also communicate using the full range of their sensory capabilities,

Below: The deep body of the copperband butterflyfish enables it to move around the reef with extreme precision.

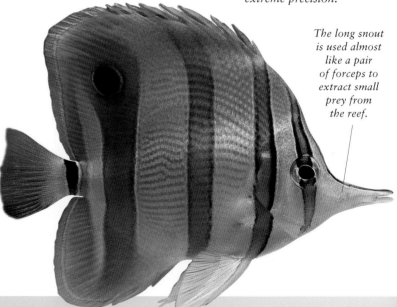

The long snout is used almost like a pair of forceps to extract small prey from the reef.

Above: The long, snakelike body of the moray eel is perfect both for hunting and for seeking refuge in the interstices of the reef.

especially smell and hearing. These are particularly important when it comes to searching out hidden prey and assessing potential mates.

Q: *How do fish use the information they gather?*

A: In common with all animals, fish are constantly gathering information on their environment. The brain receives and decodes this information and transmits a response. So if a nocturnal predator approaches under cover of dark, any surrounding prey fish may detect a large pressure

wave using their lateral line (a line of pressure sensors along the flanks). This information is transmitted to the brain via the spinal column. In response, the brain will stimulate muscles to contract, causing the fish to swim away from the direction of the pressure wave and the predator that produced it. At the same time, the fish may gather other information about the predator; for instance, it may smell it or hear if any small stones are displaced by the predator moving from concealment. Although the brain receives all this information, the fish does not have to 'think' about swimming away; moving away is a simple response.

Above: The bold colours of this harlequin tuskfish convey a signal to its own and other species.

Below: The bizarre appearance of pufferfish belies the fact that they are superbly adapted for reef life.

Communicating through colour

One of the main reasons for the popularity of coral reef fishes in the aquarium is their dramatic and dazzling colours. The underlying reason for these colours is their role in communicating messages between fish in their natural environment. Colours may change over the course of a fish's life but, to make sure each individual fish within a species is 'speaking' the same colour 'language', the signal each colour pattern conveys remains the same. Given the clarity and brightness of the water typically found on reefs, visual communication is of primary importance to the fish that live there. Coral reef fishes use colour to convey information on a variety of things, from sexual maturity to their mood, and from toxicity to the 'social' status of some species, such as cleaner wrasse, as parasite removers.

Q: Can coral reef fish change colour?

A: The colours displayed by fish are often highly variable, switching throughout their lifetimes as they mature into adults or change sex. For example, emperor angelfish change their colour patterns totally from juvenile to adult, and surgeonfish and tangs use colours to draw attention to their sharp spines. Colours also vary over shorter periods, say while camouflaged fish seek to match their background or when fish need to communicate their mood, as seahorses do, or to accentuate a display. The incredible flasher wrasses put on an amazing display during courtship, while barcheek wrasse use rapid colour changes to communicate aggression. Many fish advertise for the attention of a cleaner wrasse. Rapid colour change allows fish to communicate obviously and

effectively and, in such a visually dominated environment as the reef, it is little surprise that so many fish use it.

Q: Do the bright colours of reef fish make them targets for predators?

A: It seems obvious that a vividly coloured fish would stand out to a hunting predator, yet new research suggests that this may not be the case after all. Clearly, we cannot see the world as fish do, but from what we know of the structure of their eyes, it seems highly likely that yellow is an excellent colour for camouflage on the reef. What is more, many fish can see in the ultraviolet spectrum. In fact, it is

Below: The adult looks different, but the eyes are still masked.

Above: The dramatic livery of this juvenile emperor angelfish may play a part in directing attacks away from the head.

very likely that coral reef fishes make extensive use of ultraviolet light. The point is that fish and other reef animals see the world completely differently to us, perceiving different colours, and a prey animal that appears to us to stand out may be far less obvious to a fish predator.

Q: *How do fish create and change their colour?*

A: The colours displayed by fish are governed by

Below: To us, the lemonpeel angel appears highly conspicuous, but the blue bands are less clear.

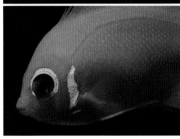

Above: In ultraviolet light the yellow fades into the background and the bands become prominent.

How fish change colour

The skin of fish contains pigment cells that overlap one another and change in response to the fish's mood to alter the way it looks.

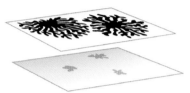

The melanophores are activated, producing a bold dark pattern on the fish's flanks.

Now the yellow/red pigment in the erythrophores has spread out and the dark pigment has retracted.

chromatophores – cells that cover the animal and contain colour pigments. There are several types of chromatophores, each responsible for a different element of fish coloration. Perhaps the most important ones are the melanophores, which contain the black pigment melanin and therefore affect the darkness of, say, a banding pattern. Melanophores, especially, are capable of rapid change in response to the fish's mood or to the environment. If these cells distribute the pigment evenly across themselves, the fish appears dark, but if the

pigment is gathered up into clumps, the skin appears lighter. Other chromatophores include the erythrophores, which hold carotenoids and affect the levels of yellow to red coloration. Iridophores, containing guanine, are responsible for the silvery shimmer of some fish. Beyond these chromatophores, reef fish may also use their protective mucus layer to accent or to hide some colours. The mucus can absorb certain parts of the spectrum, especially ultraviolet, and the fish has some measure of control over the extent of this mucus layer.

15

Communicating through behaviour

Body language – communicating with others through behaviour – is a vital part of the behaviour repertoire of all visual animals and fish are no exception. A wide variety of signals can be transmitted through body language; some are relatively subtle, but others are very deliberate and obvious. When it's important to get your message across it is best not to leave any room for ambivalence! An important facet of this is that the signals should be stereotypical – each behavioural posture should be consistent, always having the same meaning to their intended receiver.

Q: *What do fish use body language for?*

A: Much of the body language of fish is devoted to defending their own interests. When two fish such as damsels squabble, they display to one another, each holding out its fins rigidly

Below: The volitans lionfish is an expert at displaying its mood using body language. When danger threatens, it may stand on its head, exposing its poisonous fin rays.

to show the other that it is both large and in great shape. This flank display is sometimes augmented by spreading the gill covers, again to impress the rival with size (see page 146-147). Fish are usually very exaggerated and stereotypical in their aggressive displays; some enact a very rigid, almost robotic, slow swimming pattern, making absolutely sure that they can be seen by a rival. Although there are similarities between species, individuals within the same species tend to use virtually the same body

language to make sure that every 'gesture' is clearly understood. This can be quite bizarre: some species of goby adopt a display posture with their head raised and their mouth gaping open. When threatened, lionfish adopt a head-down posture. Similarly, fish at reef cleaner stations assume certain poses to encourage the cleaner wrasse or shrimp to begin cleaning them and, simultaneously, to reassure them that they carry no threat to the smaller cleaners.

Q: How do fish use behaviour to communicate fright or submission?

A: As well as informing the world at large that you are prepared to fight your corner, there are also times when dangerous aggressors must be appeased. Perhaps not surprisingly, one of the best ways to do this is to adopt a posture that is the opposite of the usual threat display. Therefore, a defensive fish will often fold its fins and do everything it can

Above: A pair of Ascension Island dwarf angelfish (Centropyge resplendens). *The male courts the female not only by displaying, but also by mouthing her flanks.*

to convince the aggressor that it poses no danger, including swimming with its head up and backing off. This latter behaviour is the most important element in communicating submission and one reason why aggression in the aquarium can sometimes continue to the death. Since a fish in the aquarium can obviously only back off so far, the aquarist needs to look out for the signals and separate the fish before it comes to this.

Q: Do fish use body language for courtship?

A: Female fish are often choosy, so males of many species have to work hard to impress their potential mates. One of the ways a male can achieve this is by displaying, helping the female to decide if he will make a good

father. In bicolour damsels, the direct relationship between the ability of the male to display and his skills and diligence as a father allows females to be sure that they are doing their best for their offspring. Male damselfish produce extensive displays during courtship to lead the female towards the nest; climbing and diving in the water column are interspersed with hovering and dipping. But displaying does not just impress potential partners, it also attracts the attention of predators; male gobies react to this by dramatically reducing their displays when a predator is in the vicinity.

Above: The male signal blenny uses its impressive dorsal fin as a warning display to deter rivals and to attract mates.

Visual contact in invertebrates

The brilliant colours of coral reef fish are matched only by those of the invertebrates that share their habitat. From soft corals to harlequin shrimps and nudibranchs, vivid colours are the rule rather than the exception. As ever, the colours are not simple embellishments, but a crucial part of the animals' anatomy that convey information to their own and other species.

Below: A row of tiny eyes can be seen along the lip of this clam's shell. Although their vision is not highly developed, clams are still able to detect the shadows of passing predators.

Q: *How well can invertebrates see?*

A: Coral reef invertebrates vary considerably in their ability to see. A great many reef invertebrates, including sponges and corals themselves, lack eyes entirely. Others, such as echinoderms, have only the most rudimentary eyes – simple photosensitive cells that enable them to detect little more than light and dark. Many starfishes are actually attracted towards the light. Bivalves, such as clams, have eyes along the opening of their mantle cavity that allow them to detect light and movement. Both are very important when

the animal is approached by a predator, such as a starfish. At the other end of the spectrum, mantis shrimps have colour vision that is thought likely to be far superior to that of humans. Cephalopods, such as octopuses and cuttlefish, are also known to have excellent sight; measuring up to 40cm across, giant squid have the largest eyes of any animal.

Q: *Why do sightless invertebrates invest in such bright colours?*

A: Even when animals cannot themselves see, they may still need to communicate to other

animals — particularly their predators, such as fish — that they are poisonous. Alternatively, colour patterns on such invertebrates can be used for camouflage. Many of the most popular reef crustaceans are very brightly coloured. As their name suggests, blood shrimps and fire shrimps are a dramatic red. Yet this helps them to blend in, because the red part of the light spectrum is quickly filtered out by water, meaning that at depths beyond a couple of metres, the shrimps appear not red but a dull green colour.

Above: The mantis shrimp (Odontodactylus scyllarus) has incredibly advanced vision, allowing it to track and capture elusive and fast-moving prey.

Changing colour underwater

Although red is conspicuous in the shallows, it can be a good colour for animals that live at depth.

Water absorbs red light so the animal appears green — good camouflage!

Q: What's special about mantis shrimp vision?

A: Although it is hard, if not impossible, to determine exactly what another animal is actually seeing, we can draw comparisons between its eye structure and our own. Human colour vision is provided by three different visual pigments in our eye's cone cells. Our eye compares what it sees to these three reference points and, from this, our brain tells us what colour we are seeing. In comparison, mantis shrimps have eight different visual pigments to provide their colour vision — they can see colours that we cannot even imagine! As well as this, the eyes of mantis shrimps are also well adapted for seeing how light is polarised and scattered in their environment. If that was not enough, each of their eyes is capable of moving independently and gaining a full appreciation of the visual field, especially depth perception. All these adaptations combine to produce perhaps the most amazing eyesight in the animal kingdom — essential for such an explosively fast predator as the mantis shrimp.

Chemical messages underwater

Animals detect the chemical cues that surround them using both their senses of smell (olfaction) and taste (gustation). Of these, olfaction is the more important, especially over long distance. Taste is used to assess things that are physically in contact with chemoreceptor cells. The underwater environment is a soup, full of chemical information about the habitat and about other animals, who is around, what they are doing, whether they are injured and so on. Aquatic animals constantly intercept these messages, choosing which they should respond to and which they should ignore.

Q: *Do fish have noses?*

A: Not exactly – but they can smell! Unlike many land animals, fish do not breathe through their nostrils, which are used solely for smell. Some species have two pairs of nostrils and actively pump water in through one pair and out through the other. As the water passes over the sensory receptors within the nostrils, the chemicals in the water flow generate nerve impulses, which may then be decoded by the olfactory bulbs situated in the front part of the brain.

Q: *How well can fish smell?*

A: A good sense of smell is essential for many freshwater fish species because vision is often limited underwater by turbid, muddy water and shade from plants, such as lilies. Coral reefs, however, are characterised by extremely clear waters. Even so, reef fishes can and do detect chemical cues. The ability is strongest in those species that live with least light. Fish in the deep seas are able to detect concentrations of chemicals as weak as one part per quadrillion. An excellent sense of smell is common to many species of fish, especially nocturnal ones.

Q: *What do fish use smell for on the reef?*

A: On the coral reef, moray eels hunt at night. They locate their prey by moving through

How the nostrils work

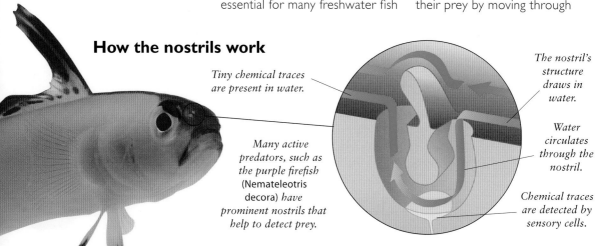

Tiny chemical traces are present in water.

Many active predators, such as the purple firefish (Nemateleotris decora) have prominent nostrils that help to detect prey.

The nostril's structure draws in water.

Water circulates through the nostril.

Chemical traces are detected by sensory cells.

Homing in on the prey

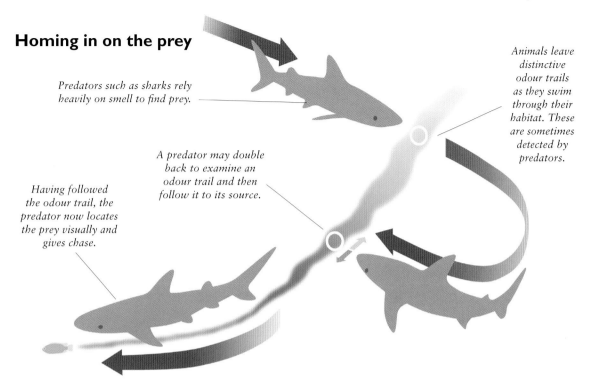

Predators such as sharks rely heavily on smell to find prey.

Animals leave distinctive odour trails as they swim through their habitat. These are sometimes detected by predators.

A predator may double back to examine an odour trail and then follow it to its source.

Having followed the odour trail, the predator now locates the prey visually and gives chase.

the holes and interstices of the reef itself, homing in on victims by detecting their characteristic odour trails in the water. Some daytime fish use their chemical senses to detect food. Goatfish, for example, use their barbels to find small invertebrates in the coral sand. These barbels are covered in sensitive chemosensory cells that allow the fish to taste its prey before it can see it. Often, fish that live along the substrate of the reef, including some blennies and gobies, also have these chemosensory cells along the undersides of their bodies.

Q: How do fish use smell?

A: The ability of fish to orientate towards (or away from) the source of an odour is called chemotaxis. Each animal produces its own odour; if a fish detects that of a prey animal, it is likely to try to use it to track down that animal. The process of discovering the source starts when the fish crosses the odour trail of the prey animal. Once the fish detects the presence of the smell, it circles to reconnect with the trail and then moves up the odour gradient, going from a weak smell to a stronger

one, until it finds the source and devours it. As well as finding food, fish are able to navigate using their sense of smell. The salmon is the most famous of all fish species for doing this, but most fish are capable of detecting and moving towards the smell of a local, familiar habitat. Each habitat has its own, unique, chemical signature and this is what the fish respond to. This ability is extremely important – fish that become familiar with a preferred area of their habitat know from experience where the best hiding places are located and where to find food.

Fish communicating through smell

Although vision is arguably the most important sense for most inhabitants of the coral reef, their sense of smell also has a key role. Odours may be detected a long distance from their source – beyond the range of an animal's vision – and can help, say, a predator locate a prey animal; for example, sharks are well known to home in on trace levels of blood in the water. When visual cues are misleading or confusing, a sense of smell can also allow animals to gather more information to help them decide what to do. Fish use their sense of smell to pick up the chemical messages passed between other animals. These chemical messages – more correctly called pheromones (from the Greek 'pherin' meaning 'to carry') – allow them to learn more about other members of their own species and to find mates. They also provide a host of other information, allowing fish to eavesdrop on their prey, their predators and indeed all the other species that share their habitat.

Q: *Over what range can smells be detected?*

A: A crucial stage in the life of a reef fish occurs when it makes the transition from a pelagic (free-living) larva to a juvenile, settled on a reef. Recent research has suggested that olfaction is extremely important in helping the larvae to find their way towards potential reefs and coral heads and to choose between them. But how do they decide which of the many options might make the best home? Many larval fish, such as humbug damselfish, are attracted towards the smell

of other members of their own species. This makes good sense on the coral reef, because if a site is suitable for them, then it is also likely to suit the larva. The sense of smell can be used to navigate accurately over smaller distances as well. For example, settling larval clownfish can detect and home in on the smell of their host anemones over several metres.

Q: How is the sense of smell used for identifying other reef animals?

A: The sense of smell is extremely important to clownfish, which lay their eggs at the base of their home anemone. While the embryos are developing, they seem to pick up the smell of this anemone and later in life, when they settle on

the reef, they show a preference for the same anemone species. They can pick up its odour over considerable distances and home in on it using their sense of smell.

Q: Is the sense of smell used in courtship on the reef?

A: Although the majority of courtship uses vision, in some species it can be triggered by smell alone. Small reef fishes are not highly mobile – they tend to spend most of their lives within a relatively small area of habitat because of the risks involved in travelling conspicuously. For this reason, the arrival of a potential mate in the immediate vicinity is an opportunity too good to miss. Often, the first clue to the presence of a new fish is its smell; male frillfin gobies, for example, are known to react strongly to female pheromones. It has been shown that chemical cues alone are enough to provoke the excitable males into performing courtship behaviours, even when they cannot see the object of their affection.

Left: Safe within the protection of the anemone, a batch of yellowtail clownfish (Amphiprion clarkii) *eggs develop under the gaze of their attentive parent.*

Invertebrate use of smell

Many reef invertebrates, especially those that lack a good sense of vision, are acutely sensitive to tell-tale chemicals in the water. Sometimes even the faintest trace, perhaps consisting of just a few molecules of a key chemical, can trigger amazing behavioural responses. Some chemical odours, such as those that carry the scent of food or mates, are especially worth seeking out; others forewarn of danger, providing any animal with a sufficiently keen sense of smell a few extra precious moments to seek shelter.

Q: *How do invertebrates detect smells?*

A: For a 'smell' to be detected by any animal, a few molecules of chemical must come into contact with specialised cells, known as chemoreceptors. There are many different types of chemoreceptor, each tuned in to a particular kind of molecule. Some chemoreceptors pick up food molecules, others detect predator molecules and so on. When a sufficient number of these molecules is detected in the water, the chemoreceptors trigger a response in the animal's brain – it smells the chemical. To acquire plenty of chemical information, animals must sample their environment. Human chemoreceptors are located mostly in our noses and mouths and detect molecules in the air as we breathe. Similarly, animals such as clams and snails have a nose-like structure, called an osphradidium, across which they can pass water, sampling it for chemicals. Crustaceans, such as

Below: The huge antennae of many prawns are covered in sensory cells that can detect the most minute chemical changes in the water around them.

shrimps, wave their antennae around in their habitat; these are covered in chemoreceptors, so they smell and taste with them. Other animals, including crabs and octopuses, are covered in chemoreceptors, making them super-sensitive to waterborne chemicals.

Q: *What do inverts use their sense of smell for?*

A: Animals use smell for four main purposes: to find a home, a mate, food or to obtain advance warning of a predator or rival. If attacked, anemones rapidly withdraw their vulnerable tentacles to safety.

If the anemone is damaged in the attack, it releases an alarm chemical to which all the other anemones in the area can respond. In addition, the chemical tags the attackers, such as predator sea slugs, making it difficult for them to sneak up unnoticed for several days. Sea slugs themselves seek out their prey, including anemones and coral polyps, by following odour trails, sniffing them out with their incredibly sensitive chemosensory abilities. Corals, meanwhile, can detect the presence of their neighbours chemically, allowing them to launch an attack if the neighbour starts to muscle in on their territory and overgrow them. Male snapping shrimps are acutely sensitive to the scent of females and use subtle chemical cues to work out whether they might be about to moult and thus be sexually receptive. The first male on the scene gets the girl, so the rewards are great. The presence of pheromones in the water is thought to be one of the key factors in triggering the mass spawning events of reef invertebrates. It seems that

Above: Despite powerful stinging cells, anemones (such as this **Heteractis magnifica**) *are targeted by some predators. If threatened, they can withdraw their tentacles.*

the spawning of the first corals on the reef acts as a signal to other corals, as well as to clams and some echinoderms, such as sea urchins and starfish. By all spawning at once, these reef invertebrates swamp the ability of predators, which feed on the rich bonanza of their eggs, to make any serious impact on their breeding efforts.

Sound detection

It is ironic that one of the early heroes of coral reef research – Jacques Cousteau – chose to call his most famous book 'The Silent World'. In fact, it is far from silent; these waters are a constant lively hubbub of noise. Recent research has shown that fish communicate extensively through sound and are capable of both producing and receiving sounds. Water is an excellent medium for conducting sound; it travels much faster (at about 1500 metres per second) and much farther in water than in air, so fish can exploit this to get their message across.

Q: *How do fish produce sounds?*

A: Fish lack a voice box and must find other means of making themselves heard. They use two main methods: 'stridulation', where they rub their teeth, spines or other skeletal parts together, and 'drumming', where muscles around the swimbladder contract rapidly and, as the name suggests, use the swimbladder just like a drum. The fishes' 'songs'

can range from the quite simple 'click', like a person cracking their knuckles, to buzzing and growling. Butterflyfish use this whole spectrum of sound during their pair bonding, including high-frequency clicks, low-frequency pulses of sound and even long and very specific series of pulses. The next step is to find out what it is that they are saying to one another!

Picking up underwater sounds

Q: *How do fish hear?*

A: Sound travels as a series of waves or vibrations through the water. Because a fish's body is a similar density to the surrounding water, the waves pass through it. However, in the inner ear there are a number of ear bones known as otoliths. Being bones, these are of a different density to much of the rest of

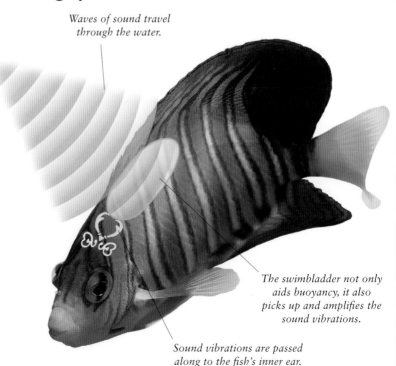

Waves of sound travel
through the water.

The swimbladder not only
aids buoyancy, it also
picks up and amplifies the
sound vibrations.

Sound vibrations are passed
along to the fish's inner ear.

the fish's body. The sound waves cause the otoliths to vibrate and this vibration is picked up by sensory cells in the inner ear and transmitted to the brain. In some species, the swimbladder amplifies underwater sounds by picking up the pressure waves of the sound. If you have ever stood near a loudspeaker and been able to 'feel' the sound, especially the low frequency bass, this is essentially the same thing. Picking up sounds is especially important to the butterflyfish, which has some remarkable adaptations to help it listen effectively. One is a unique link between the lateral line and the swimbladder; another is a highly specialised swimbladder that features both amplifying extensions and links to the skull.

Q: What are they telling each other?

A: Just as in humans, some elements of communication are intentional, while in others eavesdroppers listen in. Damselfish use different calls extensively to deter others from invading their territories. Recent research has shown that the fish are extremely good at telling the difference between individual fish, based on their calls. For instance, bicolour damsels can distinguish between strangers and the fish that hold neighbouring territories based solely on the calls that each makes – in other words, they are capable of voice recognition. The calls that males make are important in courtship as well; female damsels choose

Above: Fish are highly attuned to environmental sounds, including waves crashing on the reef and the chorus of different reef animals.

between the males at least partly on the basis of the series of different chirps and grunts they make. Fish also listen out for what their competitors are up to; if they hear other fish feeding on a different part of the reef, they home in on the sound in an attempt to join the feast. Sound is also extremely important in attracting larval fishes to reefs. Each reef has its own specific sound, produced not only by the fish that live there, but also by the currents that swirl around it and the waves that break over it, and the youngsters home in on these sounds before settling.

Chapter 2
Fish learning

To survive in the competitive environment of the coral reef, fish need to be adaptable. Those with the ability and the intelligence to learn and to adapt their behavioural strategies are the most likely to come out on top.

The image that many people conjure up when the question of fish intelligence arises is that of the goldfish's three-second memory. Yet all the evidence shows that goldfish – and indeed all species of fish – have substantially greater memory than this, as well as a remarkable capacity for learning. The fast-paced life of the coral reef presents enormous challenges for fish. Each day is a continual round of risks and rewards, where fish have to negotiate predators and competitors while seeking out mates and feeding opportunities. To succeed in such an environment, fish need to adapt and learn throughout their lives. They must memorise what constitutes a threat, where to find food and shelter and be able to recognise individual mates and rivals. Here, we will be looking at the various remarkable ways fish demonstrate intelligence, giving the lie to the old myth of fish as mindless creatures.

Q: *Can fish really learn?*

A: Yes. A basic type of learning that has been demonstrated in fishes is the ability to connect two different events. A simple example is the way that aquarium fish associate the appearance of the fishkeeper with the arrival of food. On seeing the former, the fish often begin to swim excitedly at the front of the tank, expecting the imminent addition of food. This is akin in many respects to the behaviour of Pavlov's dogs. They learned that the ringing of a bell meant that food would shortly arrive and responded by salivating expectantly. In the

Below: Reef organisms often form alliances in which both can benefit. Here, a cleaner shrimp tends its client, picking off tiny parasites and earning a meal for its trouble.

wild, fish often have to make connections between events in this way. For example, they must learn that the threatening 'growl' of a neighbouring territory-holder on the reef may precede an attack; that a drop in atmospheric pressure can foretell a storm, meaning that they should seek the shelter of deeper water; or that the presence of coral reproductive pheromones in the water means that, somewhere nearby, a food bonanza is available.

Q: *How else can fish learn?*

A: As well as this ability to learn that two events are connected, fish can also learn to associate an action with a consequence. This is exactly the same process by which performing animals, such as sea-lions, learn that if they jump through a hoop they will be presented with a food reward. On the reef, fish have learned that if they present themselves at a cleaning station, they will

(hopefully) be attended to by a cleaner wrasse or a cleaner shrimp that will pick them clean of their parasites. Another example is the way fish can learn to avoid a particular prey item because it is unpalatable, as happens sometimes when angelfish come across unfamiliar species of sponges. Fish are extremely flexible in this regard and can be taught a host of different actions and consequences in the laboratory. Scientists use this ability to study, for example, how long it takes the fish to learn under different circumstances, such as different temperatures or oxygen concentrations. By presenting them with a choice of levers to press, where only one provides a food reward, we can look at their ability to differentiate between levers based on their colour or shape. This tells us much about their evolution. Ultimately, we can also probe the furthest extent of fish intelligence to find out the limits of their ability to learn and to remember.

How intelligent are fish?

Asking how intelligent fish are is a relatively new question. It is new in the sense that until fairly recently, the general consensus was that fish had no intelligence and simply reacted to various stimuli like mindless little robots. Gradually, more evidence has accumulated from a range of different studies to suggest that, far from being brainless, fish have excellent cognitive abilities and are able to learn quickly and effectively in a wide variety of circumstances. Much of this research has concerned coral reef fishes, which have to behave adaptively in these 'cities of the sea'.

Q: *Do young fish have any in-built knowledge?*

A: A newly hatched fish is extremely vulnerable to a horde of potential predators. Recognising what can and what cannot eat you is a vitally important skill for all fish. The problem with learning is that it requires experience, yet an early encounter with a predator can be deadly, allowing no second chance and no opportunity for learning. Young fish, therefore, have an innate ability to recognise predators. This ability is not learned, but instead is encoded in the genes. It has been shown that humbug damselfish are able to recognise what does and does not present a threat. They do this by responding to certain characteristics of the fish that they encounter, particularly the configuration of their face and their size. The information they use is simple but important – large eyes and a large mouth spell danger, smaller features are less perilous, even on an equally large fish. Accordingly, vulnerable fry show less fear of the latter. It is not just the looks of a novel fish that can set off alarm bells in the minds of inexperienced fish; they also respond strongly to the behaviour of a stranger. Large trumpetfish stalk reefs hunting

Above: The small mouth of a Lamarck angel is little threat to young fish. The angel prefers smaller prey.

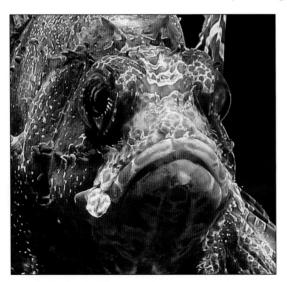

Left: The dwarf lionfish's large mouth helps small fish to recognise it as a potential predator.

for small, unwary juvenile fish, yet they are mostly ignored by their prey unless they assume their characteristic strike pose. Predatory fish often 'point' themselves towards their prey, much as a cat gathers itself before pouncing, and it is this threatening posture that the young fish respond to by fleeing.

Q: *Can fish learn through experience?*

A: Intelligence is about more than just being born with a blueprint for life encoded in the genes. To be adaptable, animals need to be able to learn. Even starfish are capable of learning

basic things: for example, new ways of righting themselves if they are overturned by an inquisitive fish or a wave surge. The living reef is home to a huge number of different organisms, some of which are worth investigating by a young fish to determine their suitability as food. But obviously these organisms (as we shall see in chapter four) are none too keen on ending up as lunch and often have quite formidable defences, including tough shells or toxicity. Fish gradually overcome these defences, improving over time as they learn through trial and error the most efficient ways of dealing with their quarry. One good

Above: The trumpetfish is an expert predator, approaching small and unwary fish using both stealth and camouflage, before striking with incredible speed.

example is the way that fish such as puffers and triggers blow a powerful jet of water to overturn sea urchins, thereby accessing their vulnerable underparts. In most cases, studies have shown that fish confronted by novel prey go from novice to peak performance over the course of approximately five episodes. This often leads to fish specialising on a particular type of prey, one they have become particularly adept at finding and eating.

Sharp minds on the reef

Exactly what constitutes intelligence in an animal is a controversial subject. It can also be a question that we regard subjectively, comparing the intelligence of an animal directly to our own, even though the animal is likely to have evolved to face very different pressures to us, pressures requiring a very different kind of intelligence. Despite this, it is true to say that long-term memory, teamwork and tool use are all hallmarks of higher intelligence and, until recently, were considered to be the exclusive reserve of animals such as primates. Remarkably, evidence now exists to show that coral reef fish have long-term memories, work in teams and even use tools.

Q: *How long can fish remember things?*

A: Once a skill or some information has been learned, it needs to be regularly reinforced, otherwise it will be forgotten. The amount of time that a new skill can be remembered is known as a 'memory window'. Contrary to common belief, memory

windows in fish can be extensive. The simplest test examined how long a fish would remember where a piece of food was hidden. Reef fish can memorise landmarks in their habitat and retain the memory for anything up to six months without it being

reinforced (see pages 36-37). They can also remember other individual fish for considerable periods; experiments suggest that individual recognition can persist between fish that have not encountered each other for more than a month.

Mobbing in reef fishes

Lizardfish are voracious predators of fish on the reef and are recognised as a danger by many species.

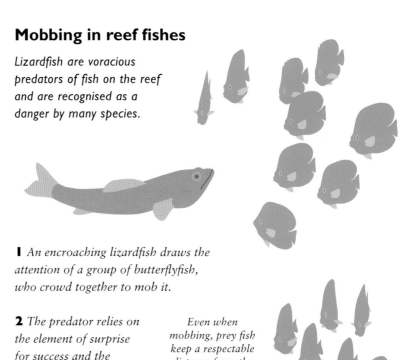

1 *An encroaching lizardfish draws the attention of a group of butterflyfish, who crowd together to mob it.*

2 *The predator relies on the element of surprise for success and the attentions of the prey group convince it to withdraw.*

Even when mobbing, prey fish keep a respectable distance from the predator's jaws at all times.

Q: *Do fish use teamwork?*

A: Teamwork is often considered to be an indication of advanced intelligence because it requires individuals to fulfil roles and to work together in a concerted way. One possible example of this in fish is mobbing behaviour, where individuals band together to harass a predator that has moved into the locality. For instance, groups of butterflyfish and surgeonfish are known to mob predatory fish such as moray eels and lizardfish. In doing this, the prey fish can prevent the predator launching a surprise attack in the first instance and ultimately drive it off. Because the many are stronger than the few, this only works if the fish team up.

Q: *How else do reef fishes show intelligence?*

A: Fishes such as the clown coris (*Coris angulata*) and the redbreast wrasse (*Cheilinus fasciatus*) pick up urchins in their mouth and crush them by ramming them into the reef. They may repeatedly use the same parts of the reef to do this, possibly in the same way that thrushes use particular 'anvil' stones to break apart the snails they feed on. The yellowhead jawfish (*Opistognathus aurifrons*) constructs its own burrow to amazingly high standards; the entrance must be precisely the right size for the fish to swim into and no larger. The burrow is built out of small stones and each must conform to the fish's exacting standards, making a perfect fit with the others around it, otherwise it will be rejected.

Below: A yellowhead jawfish (Opistognathus aurifrons) emerges cautiously from its burrow. If danger threatens, it will withdraw to the safety of its painstakingly constructed home.

Learning from others

For most of their lives, coral reef fishes live in close contact with hundreds or even thousands of other reef dwellers. There are disadvantages to this in terms of shortages of space for territories and high levels of competition for food. But there is some compensation for the fish in the way that information is quickly transmitted across the reef. Reef fishes are particularly sensitive to the signals and the behaviour of others, allowing them to learn a host of things quickly, from the location of food to the presence of predators. Sometimes that information is intended to be broadcast, at other times it is picked up by eavesdroppers – there are few secrets on a coral reef.

Q: *Where do fish get their information?*

A: All animals have their own private information, based on their own learning, exploration and experience. But gaining private information takes energy and time; to learn everything about its habitat, a fish would have to investigate huge areas of reef for itself, which would not only take time but would expose that fish to considerable danger. As a result, fish often obtain their information from watching the behaviour of others. This so-called public information is less reliable than finding things out for yourself, but it is much easier.

For example, the sounds that fish make when feeding are known to attract fish from all over the reef to investigate. In a different context, if just a few fish perform

Below: A shoal of grunts gather in a cavern. Such groups act as information centres, allowing fish to learn from one another.

a sudden fright manoeuvre, such as a dash towards the reef, this can cause others nearby to respond by copying them.

Q: Can fish learn from other fish?

A: There is plenty of evidence to show that fish can, and do, learn from one another, a process known as social learning. There are several examples of fish watching a conspecific eating a completely novel food item and then imitating the behaviour by trying the food itself. Triggerfish, such as the yellow-spotted trigger (*Pseudobalistes fuscus*) and the orange-lined trigger (*Balistapus undulatus*), are amongst the smartest fish, with several tricks that help them deal with well-defended prey, such as sea urchins. Individual orange-lined triggers in the Red Sea have been seen carefully biting off some of the spines of sea urchins before picking them up and carrying them to the water surface, then dropping them and feeding on the unprotected underside of the urchins. This behaviour is not known in other parts of the world and it seems likely that this successful innovation by an individual triggerfish has been learned by a small group of triggers.

Above: Triggerfish, such as this orange-lined trigger, are amongst the most intelligent fish, displaying behavioural flexibility and a remarkable ability to learn.

Q: Do fish have traditions?

A: Simply put, traditions are behaviour patterns that persist in populations between generations. One such tradition is seen in the migration patterns of many reef fishes between their daytime and night-time ranges. Many surgeonfish do this, but the most compelling evidence comes from a study on French grunts. When some fish were moved between different populations, they fell into step with their new associates and followed their exact migration paths, at first simply copying and later learning them. However, just because a particular resting or feeding place has been used for generations, it does not necessarily mean that it is the best one – it is tradition that keeps the fish coming back. Tests on the mating sites chosen by blueheaded wrasse showed that when two populations were switched, each going to the other's former range, the incomers chose totally different spawning sites to those used by the previous occupants, but once chosen, these new sites were maintained by the population year after year.

Finding the way around on the reef

Although a reef may look to us like a huge continuous environment, the reality for fish is much more complex. Their habitat is a patchwork of hiding places, feeding sites and fiercely defended territories. Being able to orientate within the environment is therefore a crucial skill for fishes. It is vital to be familiar with the environment – to know where food or danger may be found, where might be a good refuge or where your territory is. With so much at stake, it is not surprising that coral reef fish are expert navigators.

Q: *How do fish find their way around?*

A: Larval coral reef fishes have to find a suitable reef to settle on as they develop, yet it can be a daunting journey for such a tiny fish to make from the open seas where they spend the first few weeks of their life. Recent research suggests that they use the smell of other members of their own species to home in on likely reefs. In addition, reefs are noisy places, particularly because of the waves that break upon them, and evidence suggests that the fish also use these sounds to guide them towards the reefs. Adult fish are also thought to use these cues when migrating between different reefs that they may use for feeding and for hiding. In addition, they use familiar landmarks to orientate themselves along their route. Fish memorise landmarks on their home reef too. Experiments in the nineteenth century showed how blennies could memorise a spatial map to find their way around. More recently, a study on clownfish showed that if fish were removed from their own anemone and released elsewhere on the reef, out of sight of the anemone, they quickly found their way home, even after considerable periods away. There are even suggestions that clownfish can remember such spatial information for periods of up to six months.

Below: Clownfish, such as Amphiprion akallopisos, *are vulnerable away from the safety of their anemone and need to learn a quick route back if they stray.*

Q: *How good are they at it?*

A: Given the costs associated with getting lost, it is perhaps not surprising that fish are good at navigating. Perhaps the most dramatic example of fish finding their way around is provided by frillfin gobies. These fish are confined to rock pools at low tide and can be vulnerable to predators, such as gulls, or to the pool itself drying out. The gobies respond to these risks by jumping to a different rock pool, even though they cannot actually see where that pool is before they jump. To achieve this extraordinary feat, the gobies must memorise the relative positions of rock pools at high tide and retain this information so that they know which way to jump in an emergency. This memory extends to encompass the locations of several different rock pools, allowing the fish to leap from one to another to another in sequence. Of course, the costs of getting it wrong are great; if they miss their target rock pool, they could be stranded and die. For this reason, individuals that are captured and put into a pool without being able to investigate its location beforehand will not jump if danger threatens.

Navigation for fish

A knowledge of how to get to safety can be critical for fish, especially for those that may become trapped in tidal pools as the tide retreats.

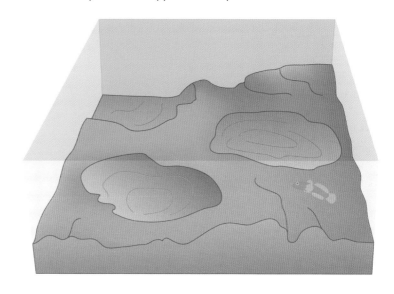

Above: When the tide is in, a patrolling frillfin goby is able to learn its way around, building a mental map of its habitat.

Below: This information can prove vital at low tide – if danger threatens, the goby can leap between pools to safety.

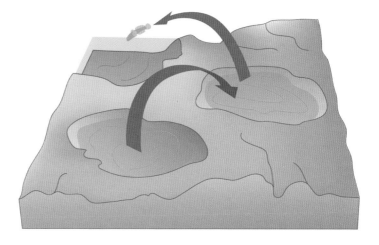

Who's who in the fish world?

The ability to recognise others is vital to fish. They have to know whether the individuals they encounter are predators, competitors or members of their own species that might potentially be a breeding partner. This recognition can be performed in a number of different ways, but the patterns and colours of coral reef fishes help to establish the identity of different species and to convey information about age, sex and dominance. As well as these visual cues, reef fish also use smell and sound to identify one another.

Q: *What and who do they recognise?*

A: As we have seen (pages 30-31), fish are extremely good at recognising what is, and what is not, a potential predator. Obviously, they also have to recognise members of their own species (a 'conspecific'), perhaps to shoal with them, or when choosing a mate. How they actually do this is not known for certain. Having spent their early life amongst the plankton, reef fishes may very well not even meet a conspecific until they

Above: Long-lived reef inhabitants, such as this coral grouper (Cephalopholis miniata), are able to recognise a variety of fishes, as well as becoming familiar with the occasional diver!

are juveniles. As we have seen (page 22), larval fish home in on the smell of adult conspecifics when settling on a reef. Fish can also tell generally what is a competitor and what is not by its behaviour (for example, grazing fish all feed in a similar way) and

by its shape and colour. But fish can also be flexible and can learn about types of fish that they have never seen before. In an experiment on this, damselfish were introduced to tilapia, a freshwater fish that they would never normally encounter. The tilapia had been acclimatised to saltwater and then trained to eat either algae (making them direct competitors to the damsels) or to eat invertebrates. Damselfish that encountered algae-eating tilapia quickly learned that they were competitors and responded aggressively, whereas those that met carnivorous tilapia simply ignored them.

Q: What other things can fish recognise?

A: Fish are capable of learning when there is a free meal in prospect. For example, it has long been known that many species of groupers keep an eye out for octopuses and moray eels, then follow them when they go hunting. In this way, the groupers can snap up prey fish that are startled out of their hiding places by the other predators. Until recently, it was thought that this was very much a one-way process and that the groupers were simply exploiting the octopuses or eels. However, it now seems that the groupers might be earning their keep by guiding the eels to the hiding places of different fish. Both coral groupers and lunartail groupers have been observed swimming up close to resting moray eels in the Red Sea and displaying to them in an unusual manner. In half the cases observed, the eel would leave its cave and swim side-by-side with the grouper, which was apparently guiding its new partner to their prey's hiding place.

Below: When moray eels (such as this spotted moray) go hunting, they often attract followers, here a butter hamlet hoping to help itself to a share of the spoils.

Getting personal

Some of the most remarkable discoveries about fish in recent years have centred on their clear ability to recognise particular individual fish. Incredible as this may seem, this capacity to distinguish specific individual identities has now been demonstrated in a huge variety of fish.

Q: *How do we know that fish recognise particular individuals?*

A: For fish that live in monogamous pairs, such as many butterflyfish and gobies, recognising your mate is clearly essential. Butterflyfish reinforce their pair bonds regularly by producing a series of different sounds. Clownfish, too, have to recognise those individuals with whom they share their home anemone. Their ability to do this is extremely impressive. After spending just one hour learning an individual's identity, they are apparently capable of recognising that fish again after one month apart, because they behave very differently towards this individual than towards a total stranger. And it is not only their mate's identity that they learn; they

Above: Clownfish, such as the common clown, tend to live in stable groups, where individual fish know every other group member.

also learn the identities of other fish within their social group, enabling them, for example, to perform appeasement behaviour to dominant individuals. However, learning identities is likely to go beyond this, even extending to members of other species,

particularly when certain individuals are encountered again and again. This enables dominance patterns to be established and maintained across the reef.

Q: *Can fish recognise one another on sight?*

A: Vision is the most important sense for diurnal (day-active) reef fish, so it is appropriate that it is used for individual recognition. Tests on recognition in clownfish showed that they are extremely good at recognising their mates and other territory members. The fish respond very differently to these familiar individuals than to strangers (they are extremely aggressive to strangers). How do they tell each other apart? Some ingenious experiments showed that the fish are using visual cues – recognising individuals by their colour patterns. To find this out, researchers gave the fish made-to-measure coats that obscured their colour patterns. They were then able to show that the fish in the coats were no longer recognised by their mates and were treated in the same way as strangers. Subsequent tests have shown that the stripes around the head are especially important in allowing individual recognition in these fish.

Q: Are the other senses used for individual recognition?

A: Fish do use their other senses to enable recognition. Their sense of smell is called into play when assessing potential mates, most especially in pair-forming fish. By sniffing their mate they are able to tell whether that fish is related to them. This is possible because each individual animal's genetic make-up gives it a subtly distinctive odour and the more similar prospective mates smell, the more likely they are to be related, meaning that they are less suitable as breeding partners. Some territorial damselfish are also able to distinguish between their neighbours simply by listening to the sounds they make, allowing them, for example, to tell the difference between an adjacent territory holder and a newcomer.

Learning your stripes

Visual recognition is the key to learning individual identities in clownfish. The fish might look indistinguishable to us, but they can tell each other apart.

Below: When researchers fitted fish with jackets that covered their stripe patterns, fish that had previously coexisted happily became highly aggressive to one another.

Right: Their jackets removed, the fish were able to recognise each other again on the basis of their distinctive stripe patterns and peace reigned once more.

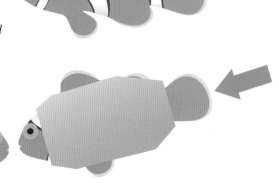

Chapter 3
Rhythms of life

Fish have three main aims over the course of their lives: to eat, to avoid being eaten and to reproduce. The way they approach these essential functions varies from species to species, but in the end, it is governed by rhythms.

Rhythms might be the short-term rhythm of the Earth rotating on its axis to produce the day-night cycle, or the annual cycle of the Earth orbiting the sun. As well as daily and annual rhythms, the different phases of the moon exert a powerful influence on the tides of the sea, which in turn affect all life on the coral reef. These different rhythms predict when fish are most active, when they eat, sleep, migrate, and when they breed.

Q: *Can fish tell the time?*

A: The behaviour of all animals on the coral reef is governed by an internal biological clock. This internal clock is set according to external stimuli known as 'zeitgebers', or 'time givers', such as the rising and setting of the sun each day or the tidal cycle. Most coral reef animals live in the tropics, where there is little annual fluctuation in day length

or temperature. Yet even in these cases, monsoon seasons can cause storms to which the fish may respond by seeking deeper waters. The biological clock starts to develop early in life. In the case of fish, it is usually almost fully developed by the time they hatch from the egg.

Q: *How accurate are these internal clocks?*

A: If an animal is taken from the wild and kept for a time in a constant environment, say, in constant light or at

a constant temperature, its rhythmic behaviour will gradually decrease in the absence of the vital zeitgebers to update their biological clocks. However, the internal clock is quite robust; depending on the species, it can take anything up to six weeks for a fish to lose its connection to the rhythms of the natural world completely. Therefore, to see natural behaviour from fish in the home aquarium, it is necessary to replicate natural day-night fluctuations and any annual temperature cycles that the fish would experience in the wild.

Left: Nocturnal fish, such as this bulleye (Priacanthus blochii) stir when their internal clock informs them that dusk is approaching and it is time to move out onto the reef.

Q: *What other rhythms do fish respond to?*

A: As well as these major influences on the rhythm of their lives, fish respond to other cycles, including the need to forage when hungry and to synchronise their activities with those of their prey and the activities of rivals or mates from within their own species. While the environment imposes its own rhythms on fish, the animals themselves also undergo a life cycle from birth to death as they hatch, grow, reproduce and die. In species with a distinct spawning season, the population is structured into year groups of different ages and sizes. In those that spawn all year round, the cycles are less clear and the community will consist of fish of all ages and sizes.

Below: Tidal rhythms have a major impact on all marine life. Here, low tide exposes the topmost corals on the reef flats at Heron Island on the Great Barrier Reef.

The coral reef during the day

The coral reef during the day is a dazzling collage of colours and activity. Huge numbers of fish and invertebrates bustle around the reef in a way reminiscent of a human city. In the tropics, day and night are of similar length, so before retiring to the relative safety of their sleeping areas, reef inhabitants have a great deal to pack into 12 hours: searching for food, fighting, dodging predators and mating.

Q: Why are most reef fish active during the day?

A: During daylight hours, the reef is flooded with bright sunlight. Fish with good eyesight can exploit these conditions to seek out invertebrate food or harvest algae when it is at its most nutritious. They are also able to spot approaching danger sooner; it can be hard for predators of reef fishes to sneak up on their quarry in these conditions. The importance of vision to diurnal fish is reflected by the bright, so-called 'poster' colours of many reef fishes, which promote species recognition and carry information variously for territorial rivals, shoalmates and breeding partners. Diurnal coral reef fishes have excellent colour vision and their eyes are protected from excessive brightness by a layer of dark pigment called melanin.

Below: During the day, when populations of reef fish are at their most dense, invertebrates must seek shelter and rely on their defences to keep them safe.

Q: When are reef invertebrates most active?

A: Many reef invertebrates, including corals, worms and plankton, are preyed upon by fish. For this reason, they tend to lie low throughout the day, waiting for night to fall before exposing vulnerable body parts in order to feed. Even sea urchins, with their forbidding spines, tend to seek shelter during the day. By retreating into tight holes and crevices on the reef, they protect their undersides, while presenting a bristling array of spines to any curious fish. Invertebrates that want to be active by day must be well protected from hungry fishes; the highly poisonous sea slugs are a good example.

Q: At what time of day do reef fishes spawn?

A: There are two daily peaks of activity for spawning in coral reef fishes. Those that broadcast drifting, pelagic eggs, such as angelfish and surgeonfish, spawn at dusk. For fish such as the Japanese angelfish (*Centropyge interruptus*), the window of opportunity is extremely narrow; these fish carry out the majority

A day in the life of a reef

Throughout the 24-hour cycle, the reef is a busy place. But animals are active at different times; while some species emerge to feed, others retreat into hiding.

Night **Day**

Large-eyed fish, such as squirrelfish, are specialised nocturnal feeders.

Large predators are a major threat at twilight.

Shoals of small planktivorous fish feed at the reef's edge.

Sea urchins feed much more actively at night.

Wrasse and butterflyfish are most active during the day.

Moray eels patrol the dark reef.

Most inverts seek shelter in the daytime.

of their breeding in a 15-minute slot straddling sunset. Spawning at this time gives the eggs the best possible chance of avoiding predators, as most of the diurnal, planktonic-feeding animals have left the water column to seek shelter by this time, and the nocturnal feeders have yet to emerge. In contrast, demersal-nesting fishes (those that lay eggs on the bottom), such as the sergeant major *(Abudefduf saxatilis)*, usually spawn early in the morning. Again, there are

generally fewer egg-predators around at dawn than later in the morning, and the eggs tend to hatch at dusk a few days later, allowing the newly emerged

embryos their best chance of escaping from the battalions of predators on the reef during the change-over period that happens every night at twilight.

Right: At midday on tropical reefs the sun penetrates the clear surface waters and creates ideal growing conditions for microscopic plants, including the zooxanthellae within the tissues of corals.

The coral reef during the day

The coral reef is an incredibly active place during the day. Fish mass over the coral heads and across the entire surface of the reef and the lagoons beyond, trying to gather enough food not only to exist, but also to grow and, in the case of adults, to produce eggs or sperm. The different types of feeders gather into specific areas; grazers and invertebrate hunters hug the substrate, while plankton-feeders head into the current to reap the drifting prey particles. But not all reef fish are active during the day; nocturnal species await the coming dusk and the start of their 'day'.

Q: When is the peak feeding time for reef fish?

A: Different feeding guilds of fish reach their peak activity levels at various times of the day. Out-and-out fish hunters can find it difficult to feed during the main part of the day when their prey is highly active and alert. Their response is to concentrate their activity to the twilight periods. Fish that forage on invertebrates, including goatfish and boxfish that forage in the sandy beds

of the lagoon and amongst the coral heads, feed more or less continuously throughout the day, starting shortly after dawn and continuing until late afternoon. Similarly, seahorses keep up a fairly steady level of feeding activity, holding on to seagrasses with their prehensile tails and snapping at tiny invertebrates as they drift past. But the availability of these prey – and of the plankton upon which many other reef fishes, including some damsels, wrasse and basslets, feed – depends to an extent on oceanic currents and the time of year. If food is abundant,

Above: Shoals of powder blue surgeonfish (Acanthurus leucosternon) *graze on the algae that flourishes under the bright tropical sun of the Maldives.*

the fish may be able to satiate themselves rapidly, then move out of the main feeding grounds in the water column and back to the safety of the reef. There, they are less at risk from the surprise attacks of fast pursuit predators, such as jacks. Herbivores, too, may feed throughout the day. However, the brightest sunlight produces the richest algae, so the best time to feed is during late

in order to spot danger early. Although these fish are resting, they do not actually sleep as we understand it. Instead, they simply conserve energy by seeking areas where there is little current to fight against and where they can benefit from the safety of the group. Similarly, moray eels spend the day hidden from view. Although they are known to emerge to forage occasionally during the day, most of their hunting is carried out at night.

Above: Fast-swimming pursuit predators, such as jacks, cruise the waters off the reef looking for stray fishes. As night approaches, they may move closer to the reef.

These tightly packed gatherings can be seen underneath coral outcrops and in underwater caves. The fish on the periphery of the shoal usually face outwards

Below: Nocturnal fishes, such as these squirrelfish (Myripristis berndti), wait out the daylight hours, packed tightly into underwater caves.

morning and early afternoon and it makes sense for the grazers to pack in as much feeding as possible at this time.

Q: What do nocturnal fishes do during the day?

A: While the brightly coloured diurnal fishes bustle around the habitat, their nocturnal counterparts spend the day concealed. Fish such as cardinalfish, squirrelfish and soldierfish that feed on plankton at night, seek shelter in huge shoals, sometimes numbering tens of thousands of individuals.

The coral reef at night

At night the coral reef is a very different place. The brightly coloured fish have sought refuge within the gaps and interstices of the reef. The clamour that characterises the coral reef day is replaced by an apparently quieter night, yet on closer observation, there is still plenty of activity. Nocturnal fish and larger invertebrates, such as octopuses, emerge from their hiding places and disperse over the reef to hunt. And for the invertebrates that rely on plankton for their food, the night provides both cover and an abundance of nourishment.

Left: The night is a dangerous time for small diurnal fishes that have failed to reach safety, as an army of larger predators, such as these snappers, move onto the reef to feed.

Q: *What are the nocturnal fishes like?*

A: Many daytime fish have their equivalent among the night-time assemblage, but these fish are very different in appearance.

They have large eyes and their vision is boosted by a reflective layer within the eye that allows them to gather as much of the faint light as possible. Even so, most nocturnal fishes have no colour vision and their sight is

The plankton migration

Marine zooplankton move through the water column, ascending at dusk to feed on phytoplankton during the night before descending again at dawn.

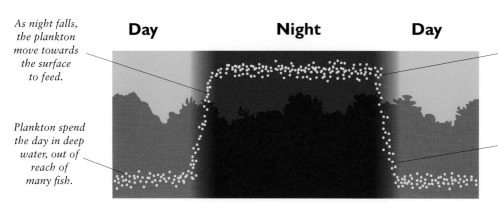

As night falls, the plankton move towards the surface to feed.

Day

Night

Day

Surface waters are packed with billions of planktonic animals at night.

Plankton spend the day in deep water, out of reach of many fish.

As day approaches, the plankton migrate back to deeper water.

restricted to shades of grey. For this reason, nocturnal fish often lack the dazzling colours of their diurnal cousins, instead relying on communication by sound; the aptly named 'drums', such as the jackknife fish *(Equetus lanceolatus)* and highhat *(Pareques acuminatus)*, are masters of this. Squirrelfishes and cardinalfishes feed on the plankton, which is far more abundant at night. At this time, grunts migrate into the reef and the lagoons beyond to feed on the emerging invertebrates. Groupers and snappers patrol the reef in search of unwary fish prey, while morays seek out the shelters of the resting diurnal fish, mainly by smell. It is thought that the mucous sac produced by parrotfish, which holds in much of the fish's odour, is an adaptation to restrict the ability of moray eels to seek them out. Reef sharks use both their sense of smell and their exquisite electroreception abilities to detect the minute electrical impulses produced by their victims in the low light.

Q: Why are so many different planktivores active at night?

A: Although there are many diurnal planktivorous fish, it is at night that invertebrate planktivores really come into their own. This is partly because many of their main predators are less active at night and partly because the plankton itself migrates over the course of the daily cycle, rising to the surface waters to feed as dusk gives way to night. Just before dawn, the plankton descend once more to the safety of deeper waters. The concentration of these tiny animals, including larval crustaceans and worms, is far higher on the reef at night, and the size of each individual animal within the plankton tends to be higher during the night than during the day. This in turn makes the night-time plankton more nutritious. This upward migration of plankton from the deep is an extremely important part of the daily pattern of life on coral reefs and supports a huge range of different planktivorous reef organisms. Individual coral polyps emerge from their limestone shelters to capture their food from this plankton bonanza. Featherstars and brittlestars scale the reef to reach good feeding spots, spreading their netlike arms to ensnare the tiny animals that drift in the water currents. Shrimps that spend the day scavenging amongst the reef join in the feast, resorting to the same sievelike appendages to harvest their food.

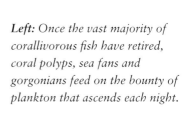

Left: Once the vast majority of corallivorous fish have retired, coral polyps, sea fans and gorgonians feed on the bounty of plankton that ascends each night.

The coral reef at night

The dark of night provides cover for a host of reef creatures, allowing them to emerge from their daytime shelters, safe from the depredations of the animals that threaten them. In many instances, the tables are turned – the diurnal hunters of invertebrates are themselves at great risk from the deadliest reef predators, including morays and reef sharks. Although this is a dangerous period for many adult fishes, it is also the time when their larvae hatch and disperse into the plankton and, later, return to settle on the reef.

Q: *Why do so many demersal-spawning coral reef fishes hatch from their eggs at night?*

A: The most likely reason is that this is when they stand the best chance of making it safely away from the reef to join the larvae of broadcast-spawners hunting in the swarms of plankton that will provide them all with both food and shelter during their early life. Damsels in both the Caribbean and in the Pacific tend to hatch in the first

hour following dusk, giving them ten or eleven hours to ride the currents away from the reef and make themselves scarce before the huge populations of diurnal adult reef fish return. Hatching is controlled by light levels; if the eggs of sergeant majors are kept in artificial light, the embryos will delay their hatching. Mouthbrooders follow the same pattern, releasing their larval young from the safety of the buccal pouch soon after dusk.

Q: *When do larval fish settle onto the reef?*

A: After their period of development drifting amongst the plankton, larval fish seek out a reef on which to settle and drift in from their offshore nursery on the ocean currents.

Below: At full moon, diurnal fish continue to feast throughout the night. Here, Chaetodon ephippium *forages for polyps after sunset.*

This usually happens at night, again to avoid the battery of diurnal fish that would pick them off easily if they attempted to settle during the day. They arrive in numbers, like soldiers storming a beach. Having reached a suitable reef, the larvae undergo a rapid metamorphosis and settle as new juveniles, a process that once again tends to occur under cover of darkness.

Q: What do adult diurnal fish do during the night?

A: For the most part, those fish that were active during the day seek shelter at night, in many cases using those places recently vacated by the emerging nocturnal fish. Nevertheless, during a full moon there are reports of some diurnal butterflyfish using the brighter conditions to continue foraging throughout the night. However, the night brings danger in the shape of high predator activity. No longer equipped to detect danger by sight, diurnal fish find themselves at a disadvantage, especially against predators that hunt by smell. Their best chance is to make themselves inconspicuous or to hide themselves well in the reef. Quite a few species achieve the former by changing colour as night sets in. Moorish idols (*Zanclus*

Above: Many diurnal fishes, such as these Moorish idols (Zanclus cornutus), modify their behaviour or colour patterns at night in an attempt to become less conspicuous to predators.

cornutus) and surgeonfish, for example, adopt more subdued, darker colours to help them blend in. Hidden triggerfish lock their dorsal spines upwards, bracing themselves against the rock of their shelter. Once wedged in, it is almost impossible for a predator to extract them. Other fish, including some wrasse, hide beyond the reef, sheltering beneath the sand itself, only to emerge as dawn breaks.

The twilight zone

Dawn and dusk are incredibly active times on coral reefs. Together, these twilight, or crepuscular, periods take up only about an hour of each day, which amounts to only about 4% of the 24-hour cycle, but they are extremely important to all reef life. This is a time of transition between diurnal and nocturnal reef species and can be a highly dangerous period; predators eyes' are well suited to the twilight. Many reef fishes spawn at dusk, thereby exposing themselves to great risk, but at the same time giving their eggs the best chance of reaching safety.

Q: *What changes happen during dawn and dusk?*

A: The daily twilight periods are when fish and invertebrates emerge or retreat to their refuges. Diurnal fish stir from their overnight resting places and swarm out onto the reef at dawn, returning to these shelters at dusk, while nocturnal fish follow the opposite pattern. At dusk, the smaller species of fish migrate down to the reef first. Some species migrate from their daytime feeding grounds to their night shelters along predictable migration routes, which can cover surprisingly long distances. In the Red Sea, brown surgeonfish

(*Acanthurus nigrofuscus*) can travel over a kilometre between these sites, using learned landmarks along the way to navigate. Often, fish return to exactly the same place to rest night after night.

Q: *How do animals know when to emerge or hide?*

A: At dusk, light levels decrease from around 100 lux just before sunset to 0.01 lux only 30 minutes later. Although the fish

Below: Pale-lipped surgeonfish (Acanthurus leucocheilus) *begin their daily migration from their daytime feeding grounds to their overnight resting spot.*

Above: *To see more natural twilight behaviour patterns amongst fish in the home aquarium, gradually shut down the lights, one tube at a time.*

use these light cues to prepare to switch their activity patterns, they are also guided by their internal clocks and start to make the transition well ahead of actual dawn and dusk. If fish in an aquarium are switched from a consistent night and day regime to one where the light is held constant over time, they will continue to switch from night to day behaviour and vice versa at the correct time for quite a few days. After this, the absence of anything to reset their internal clocks will cause the timings to go awry.

Q: What it meant by the 'quiet time'?

A: Between one set of fishes going into shelter and their counterparts emerging to feed, there is a period of about 20 minutes when the reef seems absolutely devoid of all life. This slightly eerie period is sometimes referred to as the 'quiet time'. One of the reasons for this dead zone in the reef's daily transitional period is the abundance of predators at this time. Dawn and dusk are when hunters are at their most effective, because their eyes are attuned to the half-light and this gives them the edge. Predators capture a substantial proportion of their daily food during the twilight periods. Many predators, including groupers and snappers, keep close to the reef, maintaining a watch on the waters above. Even at twilight their prey are silhouetted against the surface, while the prey themselves find it difficult to see the danger lurking against the growing gloom of the reef below. If a fish does swim above it, a predator can launch a surprise attack from below and capture its quarry before it can react.

A year round the reef

At the equator there is very little variation in day length or temperature over the course of the year. As a result, the animals that live on coral reefs at very low latitudes show few regular annual patterns in their growth or behaviour. But with each kilometre travelled north or south away from the equator, the influence of the seasons increases. Although warm weather and bright conditions are still the norm at the Tropic of Cancer and the Tropic of Capricorn, the days are noticeably longer and warmer in summer than in winter, with up to two-hour changes in day length and 10°C temperature differences over the course of the year. These differences affect the coral reef animals at higher latitudes by promoting seasonal behaviour.

Q: Do coral reef fishes breed all year round or do they have breeding seasons?

A: Perhaps the majority of coral reef fishes spawn throughout the year, taking advantage of the consistently good conditions that are found on most reefs to produce as many offspring as they can. But even amongst those that do breed year round, there are often peaks of spawning activity, when the fishes synchronise their greatest effort with ideal conditions. In the northern Red Sea, coral reef fishes experience perhaps the greatest seasonality. Here, fish make use of the warm waters of the summer months to breed. Temperature levels are extremely important for the development of both eggs and young; development and growth are faster in warmer waters. So the adoption of breeding seasons by tropical marine fishes is likely to be related both to this and to higher food availability. Also, the faster metabolism of the adults during the warmer months enables them to produce plenty of eggs rapidly, compared to other, leaner periods of the year.

Left: The Red Sea is near the northern limit of coral reefs – one of the few places where tropical marine fishes experience seasons.

Reefs around the world

The Western Indian Ocean offers ideal water conditions and, as it straddles the equator, it fluctuates little throughout the year. The Red Sea does have a seasonal influence, however.

The Caribbean Sea is home to many familiar occupants of the tropical marine aquarium. The spring spawning peak occurs between February and April in the Northern Hemisphere.

The seas off Southeast Asia and Indonesia down to Australia are rich in coral reefs. Warm ocean currents extend their range to Lord Howe Island. The further south you travel, the greater the influence of the seasons.

Q: If fish do have breeding cycles, when are these?

A: Across the globe, annual spawning peaks have been recorded in the Caribbean, the Red Sea and the Indo-Pacific. As a rule, spawning activity peaks around spring, both in the Northern and Southern Hemispheres. Caribbean fish, for example, are most likely to breed between February, March and April. It has been suggested that this is to coincide with annual peaks in plankton levels for the resulting larval fish to feed on, but this link remains unproven.

Q: How do the fish know when these seasons are?

A: Even though they are not as pronounced in the tropics as elsewhere in the world, changes in day length keep the fishes activity co-ordinated. The onset of spring stimulates them and causes them to come into breeding condition. This works because the fish have a so-called 'photoinductible' phase in their brain, making them highly sensitive to the tiny changes in daylight and day length that occur at this time of year. During spring, the days lengthen almost imperceptibly, yet the

brain registers these changes, along with the slight day-on-day increases in temperature. These cues are backed up by the spawning behaviour of many other animals on the reef. Even low levels of sex hormones in the water are thought to promote breeding activity in members of the same species or even in completely different ones.

Everything under the moon

Life on the coral reef is not only synchronised to the 24-hour cycle of night and day and to the annual seasonal changes seen most markedly in places such as the Red Sea. The orbit of the moon is also enormously important to life in the sea. It is the moon, of course, that principally regulates the tides. As it waxes and wanes throughout the course of a lunar month, it also defines important parts of the life cycle of coral reef animals of all kinds.

Q: *How does the moon affect sea life?*

A: In simple terms, ocean tides are caused by the gravitational pull of the moon and the sun. Twice each month, when there is a full moon and when there is a new moon, the alignment of the moon and the sun means that their gravitational pulls are combined and produce peak tidal ranges, or 'spring' tides. As well as the increased water currents found during spring tides, a full moon means that the reef will be bathed in moonlight. There are several documented cases of diurnal fish, including butterflyfish and angelfish, continuing to forage busily in these conditions.

Q: *How do moon phases and tides influence the behaviour of reef animals?*

A: The biggest effect of the moon phase is on spawning behaviour. Many coral reef animals show what is known as lunar or semi-lunar periodicity in their breeding efforts. In other words, their spawning peaks once every lunar cycle (usually at full moon) or twice every lunar

Above: Although the moon is relatively small compared to other celestial bodies, its proximity to earth ensures that it plays a vital role in regulating the tides.

Spawning by the moon

The moon dictates the tides of the sea, which in turn have a strong influence on the timing of fish spawning efforts. Many species hit a spawning peak at full moon and new moon.

Full moon

New moon

cycle (at full and new moon). This periodicity allows them to synchronise their behaviour with other members of the same species at ideal times for the survival of their eggs and young. As well as breeding, fish move around their habitat according to the tides. As tides fall, smaller animals move into slightly deeper water to avoid being trapped in rock pools, which can fluctuate widely in temperature and salinity. As they move, predators often wait for them, stationed along the route that their prey take as they escape. Those animals that do survive return to their shallow feeding grounds as the tide moves back in.

Q: Why do so many reef species choose to spawn at full or new moon?

A: Many of the coral reef fishes that spawn in open water dart up from the reef into the water column to release their eggs on ebbing tides. The currents then carry the eggs away from the reef and from the huge numbers of egg-predators that live there. Once hatched, the larvae often use an incoming tide to ride in to a reef to settle. The same applies to the many invertebrates, such as coral, that use a similar tactic with the moon and tide

phase. As well as using the tide to carry the spawn to safety, if many animals spawn at the same time, the huge number of eggs produced swamps the ability of predators to eat them all. This ensures that a good proportion

survive to reach the comparative safety of waters away from the reef. Across the reef, the chemical signals of breeding animals of all species stimulate others to breed at the same time, enhancing this mass spawning effort.

Time and tide

Most marine organisms are strongly affected by the tides. For some, the rising and falling waters are an opportunity, for others a hazard.

1 *As the tide starts to ebb, large fish sometimes wait along the reef edge for the receding waters to flush out hidden prey.*

2 *At low tide, animals may become stranded in rock pools, facing extreme temperatures and salinity under the baking sun.*

3 *With the tide flowing, the top of the reef is submerged once more. Fish can feed and animals stranded in pools can make their escape as waters rise.*

The fish and the egg

Fish begin life inside an egg. As we have seen, for many coral reef species the exact moment of fertilisation occurs in the water column amidst a swarm of predators – not the easiest start in life! From this point on the pace of development is relentless; eggs are an excellent and nutritious food source for a huge number of different predators and it is a race for each developing embryo to hatch before it is found and eaten.

Below: Queen angelfish may produce thousands of tiny eggs at each spawning. Despite their size, the eggs develop and hatch rapidly.

Q: *How long does it take for an egg to hatch?*

A: There is quite a range of hatching times among coral reef fishes, but they fall into two basic categories: fish that spawn in the open waters produce eggs that hatch rapidly, whereas the eggs of demersal spawners can take several days. For example, the eggs of larger, pelagic, broadcast spawners, such as queen angelfish, hatch in 15-25 hours depending on temperature. By contrast, the comparatively large eggs of demersal-spawning clownfish take around one week to hatch in some species, again depending on temperature.

Q: *Why does the hatching time depend on temperature?*

A: Almost all fishes are poikilothermic – in simple terms, cold-blooded – so their body temperature, and therefore their metabolic rate, depends on the temperature of the water they live in. Inside the egg, the rate of development depends on water temperature in the same way. Within the normal temperature range, the warmer the water, the faster the egg develops.

Q: *How does predation affect hatching times and numbers?*

A: Predation on the free-floating eggs in the plankton layer of species such as angelfish is extremely high. Each day, about a third of all the eggs are eaten. Over evolutionary history, fish have responded to this by laying more and more eggs, and many broadcast-spawners produce tens or even hundreds of thousands of tiny eggs. The eggs of *Centropyge* angelfish are only around 0.7mm in diameter. Even in such large numbers, the eggs themselves are defenceless.

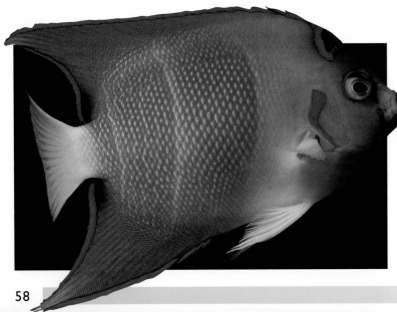

Eventually differentiation occurs – cells are guided by genes to form specific tissues and organs and the nervous system and the brain develop. Shortly before hatching, tiny muscles are twitching, the heart is beating and eyes are clearly visible. The embryo is almost ready to hatch. It is curled tightly around the yolk sac, so the egg now offers little room for further growth. The next stage of life occurs in open water.

Below: Rapid development inside the egg means that the larvae use up a great deal of oxygen. Parental clownfish fan their eggs to maintain oxygen supplies.

Above: Demersal-spawning fish, including coral gobies (Gobiodon sp.), produce fewer and larger eggs than broadcast spawners. Their eggs also take longer to hatch.

Although a newly hatched larva could scarcely be described as well protected, it can at least move around and its ability to avoid predators improves with every passing day. Therefore, rapid hatching is likely to be an adaptation to reduce the risks of being eaten. Thanks to the attention of their parents, egg mortality is much lower in demersal spawners, so they develop at a more leisurely rate.

Q: What's going on inside the egg during development?

A: Each egg is a complex chemical mix of proteins, fats and sugars, plus a genetic code to fit them together, all contained within a protective, but permeable, shell. Fertilisation is the starting point for an incredibly frantic period of activity in which a single cell develops into a functioning animal in mere hours. At first, the cells divide to produce identical copies of each other – one becomes two becomes four becomes eight and so on.

Larva life

When the embryo hatches from its egg and begins the next stage of its life as a larval fish, the pace of its development remains rapid. The odds of it surviving past the larval stage are still tiny, but to have any chance at all it needs to grow – and quickly. Eggs released into the water column are carried out on ebbing tides to hatch in the open seas, while those that spent the egg stage in their parent's nest also drift out to sea on currents as they hatch. So for almost all reef fish, the larval stage of life occurs away from the reef itself and, therefore, away from the armies of potential predators that exist there. In many cases, the newly hatched larvae lack fundamental structures, such as fully developed sensory systems, fins and digestive tract, which can take two to three days to develop. Gradually the fish is 'wired up'; its senses and its movement become more co-ordinated, it becomes better able not only to hunt, but also to avoid its predators. Even so, the continuing danger drives the pace of their development.

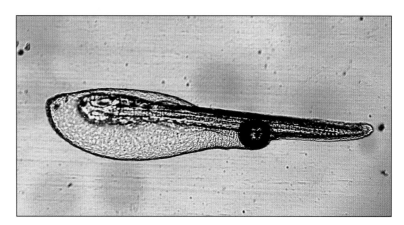

Above: At 16 hours, the larva of the resplendent angelfish, in common with the larvae of many tropical marine fish species, is barely recognisable as a fish.

Q: Do the larvae just drift randomly in the sea?

A: It was originally thought that larvae dispersed over long distances, but recent research suggests that this may not be the case. A study that tracked the movements of individually marked larval ambon damselfish (*Pomacentrus amboinensis*) showed that up to 60% of the larvae returned to the same reef and the same population as their parents. As well as this, it seems that some fish miss out the pelagic stage altogether and undergo the larval stage of their development in the lagoons of their own reefs, remaining close to where they were spawned.

Q: How long do fish spend as larvae?

A: The exact amount of time varies according to species, temperature, food and the need of the larvae to find a good place to settle. Clownfish and other parentally guarded species spend amongst the shortest periods of time as larvae – perhaps as little as one to two weeks. One possible reason for this is the larger size of their eggs and the longer period the embryos spend developing inside them. Open water spawners, such as angelfish, usually spend considerably longer as larvae. Some of these fishes spend up to 20 weeks at the larval stage before settling.

Q: Do the larvae look like their parents?

A: In the pelagic stages, reef fishes are very different morphologically from the benthic (bottom-dwelling) adults, because reef fish larvae do not hatch fully developed. For a start, the eggs and larvae are small. The larvae also need different morphological features for their pelagic existence, such as defensive spines and bony plates for protection, and large eyes and mouths for hunting. Larval Atlantic blue tangs (*Acanthurus coeruleus*) look so different to their parents that they were once thought to be a totally separate kind of fish and were named *Acronurus*. The larvae of butterflyfishes, known as tholichthys, also bear little resemblance at this stage to what they will later become.

Q: How do the larvae find their way to a suitable reef?

A: The larvae of most species ride back inshore on an incoming tide at night. To find their way to a good reef they are guided by both sounds and smells. Each reef has a characteristic sound, produced by a combination of wave patterns over the coral heads and a so-called 'nocturnal chorus' of feeding invertebrates. The larvae also use chemical cues to locate a good reef and are strongly attracted to the smell of adult conspecifics (see page 22).

A tang takes shape

At each successive stage of their life, fish such as the blue tang face different pressures. This fact is reflected in their appearance, which can change considerably as they grow and develop.

A late-stage blue tang larva (Acanthurus coeruleus) *is almost completely transparent, helping to make it inconspicuous to predators.*

Juvenile blue tangs are, perhaps confusingly, bright yellow. While this may seem to make them stand out, yellow is actually a good colour for camouflage on the reef.

As the fish matures into adulthood, it develops the rich blue colour that gives the species its name.

Settling on the reef

Less than 1% of the fish that started their journey through life inside the egg survive to settle on a coral reef as a juvenile. These larvae come inshore to the reef, guided by its smells and sounds, often borne on incoming tides and under cover of darkness. Yet even for those that make it this far, life remains hazardous and they face a difficult fight for a place in the crowded fish community on the reef itself.

Q: How does the fish change when it becomes a juvenile?

A: The transition from larva to juvenile involves some significant changes in appearance, diet and lifestyle. For example, the blue tang *Acronurus* larvae change over the course of about a week from a silvery colour to brown. They become more rounded in shape and develop their characteristic snout. They also gradually lose the spines that previously protected them in the plankton. Then at about 5cm long, the juveniles finally settle onto the reef. Throughout the larva-to-juvenile period, growth remains extremely rapid, but there are

considerable differences between species in the size of these newly settled juveniles. Some species, such as parrotfish, settle when they are only one fiftieth of the size of fully grown adults. Others, such as some gobies, are almost fully grown at this time.

Q: Why are so many juvenile fish a different colour to the adults?

A: Juvenile fish tend to have different colour patterns to adults. The reason for this is that, in the wild, a small, brightly coloured fish is unlikely to survive to adulthood; some

colours may attract either predators or aggression from mature adults. Quite a few juvenile reef fishes, including some surgeonfish, are bright yellow as juveniles. Although this might seem an unusually bright and conspicuous colour to us, recent research suggests that, from a reef fish's perspective, yellow is actually quite a good colour for blending into the background.

Below: The seachub (Kyphosus cornelli) *changes its diet as it grows, switching from being an invertebrate predator to being herbivorous, grazing on algae.*

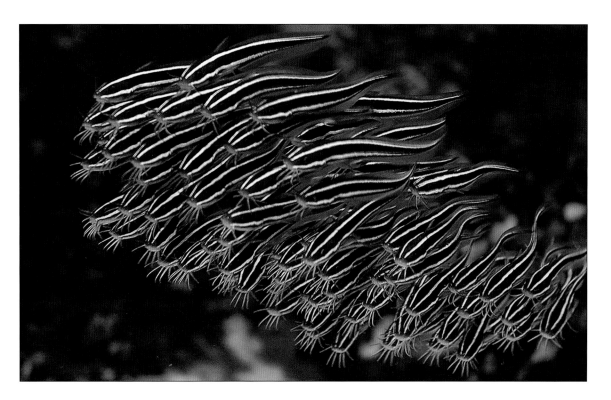

Above: Juvenile marine catfish gather into tight groups as they search for food. The shoals are said to change shape to imitate underwater objects in order to confuse predators.

Q: How do juveniles cope with the intense competition on the reef?

A: Carving out a niche in the fiercely competitive environment of the coral reef is never easy for a newly settled juvenile. They are disadvantaged by their small size, as well as their need to remain close to the refuge of the reef. Some species that in later life live a solitary and territorial existence, shoal as juveniles. An example of this is provided by the marine catfish *(Plotosus lineatus)*, which aggregate together in extremely tight groups when young, only to abandon this strategy as they grow. Shoaling enables them to break into the territories of larger fish, as well as giving them protection from predators. Another useful strategy that some juveniles use while becoming established on the reef is to have a different diet from the adults, thus avoiding direct competition. Many adult fish that live exclusively as grazing herbivores are at least partially carnivorous as juveniles. This is the case in the seachub *(Kyphosus cornelli)*. At first, juveniles feed on small reef invertebrates and plankton, but gradually switch to a more herbivorous diet as they grow. During this time their digestive system alters to accommodate the changes in diet, and the bacteria that will later help them to digest algae start to colonise the gut.

The winners of life's lottery

The final stage in a fish's life cycle is adulthood. To reach this point, each individual fish must have overcome virtually insurmountable odds with a combination of good luck and good genes. They needed good luck in the earliest part of their existence as eggs and larvae, and good genes to provide them with the armoury necessary to hunt effectively, avoid predators and win a place amongst the community of the reef. Finally, at this stage, the fish will get their chance to pass on those genes to their own offspring.

Q: *What changes accompany the transition from juvenile to adult?*

A: The transition from juvenile to adult comes when the fish reach sexual maturity. Their appearance changes, males and females become easier to tell apart and they often advertise their maturity through colour patterns. Breeding adults are often far more colourful than juveniles, and adult males are sometimes more colourful than adult females. But just as adulthood can change the way

Above: Fish seldom live to old age unless they are kept in captivity, like this grouper in a Thai public aquarium. Although growth slows dramatically, it never actually stops, so very old fish can be huge!

that fishes look, it also changes how they behave. As juveniles, fishes' main concerns are to find food and avoid predators, but once they reach adulthood, reproduction goes straight to the top of their list. As a result, fish often become more aggressive

as they seek to stake their claim, especially with members of their own sex. They may also start to defend territories and attempt to court potential mates.

Q: *Does reaching adulthood represent the last developmental stage?*

A: Not always; many reef fishes, such as clownfishes, reach maturity as males and later change to being females (known as protandry, see pages 166-167).

Others, such as many wrasse species, mature into females before developing into males (protogyny). This is discussed further on pages 164-167.

Q: How long do reef fishes live?

A: The length of a fish's life is usually related to its maximum size. The smallest fishes often live fast and die young. The ever-present threat of predation means they cannot afford to hang around; they must mature early and breed rapidly. By contrast, larger fish, such as some groupers, may live for well over a decade. The fish with the shortest lifespan is the pygmy goby *(Eviota sigillata)*, found on the Great Barrier Reef. It lives for no more than two months, only about three weeks of which is spent as a mature adult. As fish approach maturity their growth slows, although it never actually quite stops. Fish show what is referred to as 'indeterminate growth', so in fact the concept of a maximum size is slightly misleading. Although it can be difficult to determine the exact age of a fish from its size, older fish often have a typically hunched back, caused by their muscles tightening with age. However, few fish manage to achieve anything like old age in the wild, so although theoretically many species can live for several years, perhaps less than one in a million of those that start out as eggs actually does.

Below: The pygmy goby is the shortest-lived vertebrate. It packs a lot into its brief life: growing, feeding and breeding before senility sets in at the age of 60 days.

Chapter 4
Eating on the reef

All animals must find food in order to maintain an energy supply to fuel their metabolic processes. Each individual faces competition for scarce food resources; only those that are consistently successful are able to grow and, in turn, reproduce.

Finding sufficient food is not just about being able to fight for a share when rich pickings are on offer; it is also about innovating and diversifying – trying new kinds of food and exploiting untapped resources. The intense competition for food on the reef is one important reason why the animals there are so diverse. Reef inhabitants have radiated to fill every available niche, resulting in the formation of complex food webs.

Q: *What is a food web?*

A: A food web is a way of depicting the trophic (nutritional) processes in an environment. Simply put, it shows how each living thing links to others according to what it eats and what, in turn, eats it. Food webs almost always have plants as their foundation. Plants use energy from the sun to photosynthesise – the process by which sunlight

and carbon dioxide are converted to oxygen and energy in the form of sugars. When the plants are eaten, this energy is passed up the food chain. But at each level, organisms use energy to fuel themselves, so only a portion of the energy is passed up the food chain, meaning that

there is a limit to the number of levels that can exist in a food chain before the energy runs out.

Below: The coral reef community teems with activity as each animal competes for access to the incredible wealth of food to be found in these shallow waters.

Reef food web

Marine food webs are usually more complex than those found on land – none more so than on coral reefs.

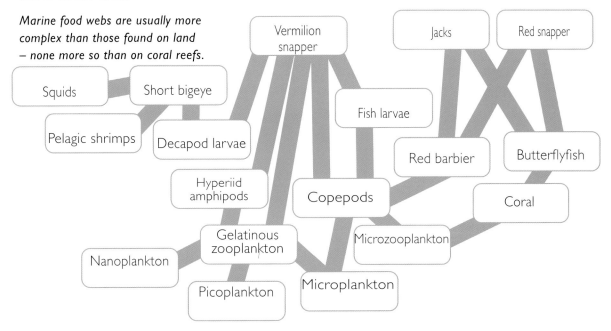

Q: *What does the coral reef food web look like?*

A: The coral reef food web is supported at the bottom by single-celled plants known as phytoplankton. These are invisible to the naked eye; you could fit several thousand of them side-by-side in the space of a single millimetre. The phytoplankton live in the well-lit surface waters and are in turn eaten by microscopic animals called zooplankton. Thousands of species fall into this grouping, including both animals that spend all their lives

in this stage and others, such as the larvae of larger animals, who are temporary residents of the plankton during their early lives. There is a whole food web within the zooplankton; some species graze on the phytoplankton, others actively hunt other zooplankton. Tiny crustaceans known as copepods are the most common herbivores and make up almost 75% of the zooplankton. As well as zooplankton, large numbers of fish, clams, urchins, crustaceans, snails and echinoderms on coral reefs graze on phytoplankton and the

algal turf that forms over reefs. A wide variety of reef animals, including the corals themselves, feed directly on zooplankton and then form the diet of carnivores of all kinds further up the food chain. However, things are not that simple. Some animals, such as fish, not only eat zooplankton, but are zooplankton larvae in early life. Others change their diet as they grow, so that one species can occupy more than one position within the same food chain. Thus, a well-known feature of coral reef food webs is their complexity.

Fish diets in the wild

Over tens of thousands of years, fish have evolved to be expert foragers, feeding on a huge range of different food sources, both animal and vegetable. Some have become specialists on a certain kind of food, others are opportunists, feeding on whatever they can. One thing all species have in common is that they are experts in spotting an opportunity and hunting out their next meal. Fish are the dominant vertebrates of coral reefs. About 70% of reef fish species are carnivorous, 20% are herbivores and 10% are omnivorous, meaning they have a varied diet that includes both animal and plant matter. This simple division into meat-eaters and vegetarians can be clarified by dividing the fish into so-called feeding guilds.

Q: What is a feeding guild?

A: A feeding guild is a way of grouping different species of fish according to their diet. In many cases, fish within a feeding guild are similar in appearance. Fish that browse on small reef invertebrates often have deep bodies, making them highly manoeuvrable, for example. As well as body shape, the mouthparts and teeth of fish within a guild are often quite similar, yet quite diverse between different guilds. For example, the rasping teeth of algae-eating surgeonfishes and damselfish are quite different from the amazing beaks of parrotfish or the fangs of a moray eel. The major feeding guilds of reef fishes are shown in the table on page 69.

Q: Why are so many coral reef fish so specialised in their diet?

A: The pressure of food competition on the reef has led to many species of fish becoming extremely specialised in their diet. These specialisations can

Above: By following its planktonic prey into the shallows, a shoal is itself in danger of predation.

Sifting for food

Many fish feed on tiny planktonic animals in the water column.

By rapidly opening and expanding the mouth, the fish sucks in a gulp of plankton-filled water.

The mouth is then closed, forcing the water through sievelike gill rakers that catch the plankton.

be seen in their appearance: the beaks of coral-eating parrotfish, the long snouts of plankton-eating seahorses and pipefish, and the enormous mouths of predatory groupers are all examples of this. The advantage of being a specialist is that the fish gain a competitive edge. They become expert at finding and catching their particular prey, so much so that they can easily out-compete a generalist. The downside is that their diet becomes increasingly inflexible. As an analogy, a racehorse can easily outrun any other breed of horse, but is useless for any other kind of work.

This dietary specialisation presented real problems to aquarists in the early years of tropical marine fishkeeping as they struggled to supply an adequate diet. But although fish might often be specialised for a particular type of diet, this does not necessarily mean that they will turn down the chance of a change from time to time. Fishes such as spiny chromis and sergeant majors feed opportunistically in this way, switching from a diet of mostly algae to take advantage of the annual mass spawning of corals on the Great Barrier Reef to gorge themselves on the rich pickings available at this time.

Coralfeedingguilds

Fish can be separated into feeding guilds according to their typical diet as adults, as this table shows.

Guild	Examples	Wild diet
Planktivores	Cardinalfish and bank butterflyfish (*Chaetodon aya*)	Plankton
Herbivores	Surgeons and tangs	Algae
Benthic carnivores	Grey triggerfish and wrasse	Crabs, snails and shrimps
Epibenthic browsers	Spotfin butterflyfish	Corals and bryozoans
Generalised carnivores	Hogfish, toadfish and groupers	Fish and inverts
Piscivores	Trumpetfish, morays and lionfish	Fish

Above: *Moray eels are extremely proficient predators of other fish, emerging at twilight to hunt for their unsuspecting prey.*

Lunch for larvae

Although reef fishes fill specialised feeding niches as adults, their diets are very different during their early life. At this time, almost all coral reef fish species have a pelagic stage, which is spent in the surface waters of the open seas, away from the reef. The larvae live amongst the plankton, feeding voraciously and growing rapidly.

Q: *What do the larvae eat?*

A: Newly hatched larvae are extremely small – angelfish measure only about 2mm when they first emerge from the egg. At this size the fish are limited by the size of their mouths and can only tackle the very smallest foods, including phytoplankton such as diatoms and dinoflagellates. As they grow, so does their ability to overcome larger prey and they switch to zooplankton, such as copepods and amphipods.

Q: *How do larvae hunt?*

A: Theoretically, the tiny size of larval fish makes it difficult for them to move around in their environment. At just a few millimetres long, pushing through the water must be like swimming through treacle. Nevertheless, size for size, these larval fish are the fastest swimmers in the fish world, covering up to 20 body lengths per second as they pursue the drifting zooplankton. Their mouths are often huge in relation to their bodies, far larger than when compared to the adults. These huge mouths allow them to hunt the most profitable prey and to pack on weight – many grow by as much as a third of their own body weight each day. The ability to hunt well is crucial; at this size, fish are extremely vulnerable to almost all predators and can only escape this threat by growing. Moreover, tiny fish have virtually no fat reserves and even a short period without food can be fatal. Living in the midst of a huge food swarm means that this is not usually a problem; studies suggest that starvation is not generally a difficulty encountered by free-living fish larvae. In the aquarium,

▶ Fry food

In the early years of the tropical marine aquarium hobby, breeding reef fishes successfully was a major problem. Many newly hatched fishes have virtually no reserves and quickly starve if unable to find food.

Right: The availability of cultured phytoplankton as a first food for newly hatched reef fishes has been a breakthrough for hobbyists.

managing to feed captive-bred larvae was once the greatest obstacle to propagating fish successfully, but the increasing availability of specialist products in aquarium shops means that the problem is rapidly becoming a thing of the past.

Q: How does the diet change when larvae settle onto the reef as juveniles?

A: As the larvae migrate onto the reefs and begin the transition to juveniles, their diets generally change quite substantially, moving from zooplankton to a wide range of benthic foods. Some species, including butterflyfish that subsist entirely on coral as adults, switch immediately to a diet of coral polyps, even at this early stage. Juveniles of related butterflyfish species, such as the raccoon butterflyfish (*Chaetodon lunula*) and the threadfin butterflyfish (*Chaetodon auriga*), prey on the tentacles of polychaete worms before making the transition to coral eating. Some herbivores continue to eat invertebrates after settling and then switch to algae as they grow. In addition, juvenile fish predators often augment their diet with a range of smaller reef invertebrates until they are sufficiently large to hunt successfully for fish.

Shape-shifting

Juveniles and adults of many fishes look so totally unlike one another that for many years people believed that they were separate species!

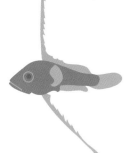

Stage 1 *This grouper larva has huge spines that make it hard to swallow.*

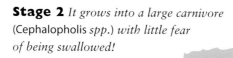

Stage 2 *It grows into a large carnivore* (Cephalopholis *spp.*) *with little fear of being swallowed!*

Stage 1 *A newly hatched unicorn tang is a hunting and eating machine, with a large mouth, belly and eyes.*

Stage 2 *As it grows, the larva develops protective spines that serve to deter predators.*

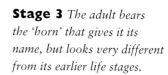

Stage 3 *The adult bears the 'horn' that gives it its name, but looks very different from its earlier life stages.*

Sunlight – the food web starts here

The shallow sunlit waters provide the perfect conditions for plant growth. The algae provide a rich and solid foundation to the food web on the reef, supporting a wide range of herbivores. But one of the most important groups of organisms on the reef are the specialised algae known as zooxanthellae that live in a symbiotic partnership with the corals and help to maintain the health of the reef itself.

Below: When food is abundant and predators are scarce, coral polyps emerge to feed in huge numbers, presenting a formidable barrier to their planktonic prey.

Q: *How does the partnership between algae and coral work?*

A: In the simplest terms, the corals provide a home for the zooxanthellae within their tissues. Furthermore, the waste products of the coral polyps also feed the tiny algae. In this secure and well-supplied environment, the zooxanthellae prosper and huge numbers of these microscopic plants are packed into coral tissue, helping to determine the colour of the overall coral. In return for their accommodation, the zooxanthellae supply the coral with oxygen and sugars as they photosynthesise. The

The coral polyp

Coral polyps catch food directly and are fed by their algal lodgers.

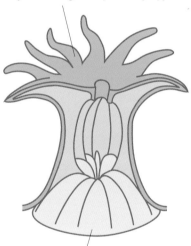

The exposed layers of the polyps are rich in symbiotic algae, which produce sugars to feed the polyp.

The polyp can withdraw its vulnerable body to the safety of its limestone skeleton if threatened.

relationship between these organisms is a long-standing one but not unique – similar relationships exist between various symbiotic algae and animals such as jellyfish, giant clams and sponges. During periods of the year when sunlight is especially bright, the corals even protect their algal guests with screening pigments.

However, if conditions become especially harsh for long periods of time, the stressed corals expel the algae. This phenomenon is known as coral bleaching and very often corals do not recover from it.

Q: *How else do corals feed?*

A: The contribution made by the zooxanthellae to the coral's overall nutritional requirements varies between coral species, but in some cases, the algae may provide up to 75% of the coral's needs. However, the coral polyps are capable of feeding themselves. Each polyp in a colony can function like a miniature anemone, trapping drifting zooplankton in the water with poisonous stinging cells resembling miniature harpoons or, in some cases, with sticky mucus. Then they retract their arms and pass the prey into their mouths. Most of this feeding is done at night, when the zooplankton are most abundant and the coral predators – diurnal fish such as butterflyfish – are gone from the reef. With this, and the daytime photosynthesis of the algae, the coral polyps have a round-the-clock feeding system.

Q: *Are other kinds of algae found on the reef?*

A: Algae forms the foundation of the coral reef food web. These tiny plants are present as free-floating phytoplankton in the water column and as the encrusting algae that grows over the reef itself. Phytoplankton are one of the major foods of the zooplankton and, ultimately, the larvae of reef fishes and invertebrates. The encrusting algae form a thin covering over the sunlit structures of the reef, where they are extensively grazed by a host of different herbivores, from urchins to tangs. The algal covering, sometimes called an algal turf, may be composed of one or a combination of different types of algae, including red, green, brown and blue-green – and is itself home to communities of tiny invertebrates and bacteria.

Stinging for their supper

Although in many cases over half of the coral's energy needs are supplied by their symbiotic algae, polyps are still capable of feeding themselves. They do this by using stinging cells known as nematocysts.

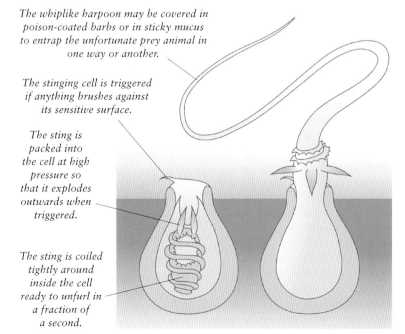

The whiplike harpoon may be covered in poison-coated barbs or in sticky mucus to entrap the unfortunate prey animal in one way or another.

The stinging cell is triggered if anything brushes against its sensitive surface.

The sting is packed into the cell at high pressure so that it explodes outwards when triggered.

The sting is coiled tightly around inside the cell ready to unfurl in a fraction of a second.

Salad days

The bright sunshine of the tropics is great news for the group of mainly microscopic plants called algae. They prosper, especially in shallow waters, and as they photosynthesise, they produce sugars that attract herbivores to feast on them. Some species of algae grow as a covering on underwater substrates, but others, such as diatoms, live freely in the water column. Each type is food for reef animals, some of which have become highly specialised to reap this rich harvest. Compared with other marine environments, coral reefs have more than their fair share of plant-eating fish, and although only around one in five of these species is herbivorous, as many as half of all fish on a reef, measured by weight, may be herbivores.

Q: Which coral reef species eat the algae?

A: There are plenty of different types of herbivorous fish on coral reefs, including surgeonfish and representatives from other families – there are algae-eating damsels, blennies, butterflyfish

Left: Urchins are extremely important browsers of the algal turf on reefs, but can create enormous damage at high densities.

Aristotle's lantern

Urchins clip away at the surface algae using intricate mouthparts – known as Aristotle's lanterns – hidden away on their undersides.

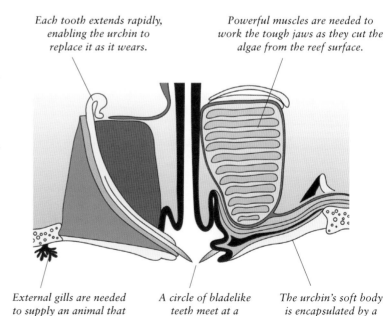

Each tooth extends rapidly, enabling the urchin to replace it as it wears.

Powerful muscles are needed to work the tough jaws as they cut the algae from the reef surface.

External gills are needed to supply an animal that lives inside a hard case.

A circle of bladelike teeth meet at a central point.

The urchin's soft body is encapsulated by a tough outer shell.

and angelfish. Compared to other food sources, algae is fairly low in nutrients, so grazing fish have to spend a proportionately greater amount of their day eating. Fish are not the only herbivores on the reef, either. Amongst the invertebrates, sea urchins are perhaps the most important of the grazers, along with a range of snails, shrimps and even some hermit crabs.

Q: *What adaptations do these herbivores have for their diet?*

A: Grazing fish usually have deep, laterally compressed bodies and strong pectoral fins that allow them to manoeuvre around the reef and to hold station while they graze on the algal turf with their tails raised. These fishes usually have fairly small mouths and bite their food off the substrate with small, incisorlike, flat-edged teeth. Many carnivorous fish, on the other hand, suck in their food and then grind it up with the pharyngeal teeth found at the back of the mouth. To extract the most from their food, many herbivores have bacteria in the gut that help to break down the otherwise indigestible parts of the algae. Sea urchins rasp at the algal turf in a similar way to the

fishes, although their mouth and tooth structure is very different. Snails, too, rasp at the algae with a specialised tonguelike structure called a radula, which scrapes against the substrate like a biological belt sander.

Q: *What is the effect of herbivores on the algae?*

A: The pressure on algae is intense. On shallow reefs, it has been calculated that herbivores make over 100,000 bites every day on every square metre of the substrate. In the process, the grazers can remove virtually all the algae that grows there. It might seem to be bad news for the algae, but this is not entirely true. On reefs where for one reason or another there are

few herbivores, the algae grows unchecked into thick, covering layers. In these conditions, a handful of algae species take over, driving all others out of the habitat. Grazers have the effect of preventing these dominant algae species from taking over, allowing the other algae species to keep a foothold. The grazers benefit as well; the dominant algae species are amongst the least nutritious, so by keeping them in check and creating the conditions that allow other species to grow, the algae as a whole provides them with a better meal. (See also page 136.)

Below: Coral reefs are home to huge numbers of herbivorous, algae-browsing fish. Here Acanthurus pyroferus *grazes the thin algae layer covering the reef.*

Eating the reef

Coral reefs are by far the largest animal-built structures on Earth. The Great Barrier Reef stretches for nearly 2,400km and is even visible from space. Nevertheless, most of the coral reef is dead, composed of the skeletons of individual polyps. Only the superficial layer of the reef is alive and this living skin represents a nutritious source

Below: The beak of the parrotfish is formed by individual teeth that are fused together. The fish is able to take bites of the reef itself!

of food for any animal that is able to exploit it. During the day, when many reef animals are grazing, the polyps withdraw to the protection of their limestone shelter, but this is not always enough to guarantee their safety.

Q: *How do parrotfish get past the coral's defences?*

A: Parrotfish are so-called because their fused teeth give their mouths a beaklike appearance. These teeth are situated outside the jaw bones,

so the beak protrudes beyond the mouth. This is perfect for scraping algae from the surface of rocky substrates, but can also get past one of the algae's defences – growing within the matrix of the coral itself. In some species, such as the hump-headed parrotfish, the beak can take a chunk out of the reef itself. Interestingly, although the parrotfish eat the polyps themselves, these herbivorous fishes are probably primarily interested in the zooxanthellae contained within the coral's tissues, rather than the coral itself.

Q: *How do the parrotfish eat such a rocky diet?*

A: To counteract their tough diet, parrotfishes' teeth grow continuously. But those that form the beak are not the only teeth that these remarkable fish have; the platelike pharyngeal teeth towards the back of the mouth can bring considerable crushing force to bear, pulverising even the tough limestone. After this, the coral's resistance is at an end. In the fish's gut, living tissue is separated from the limestone rubble and powder. This ground material is ejected by the parrotfish as fine, white grains, which makes up a considerable proportion of the highly prized white sand found in coral reef lagoons and beaches!

Q: *What other predators threaten the coral?*

A: Although the damage done by parrotfish can be quite dramatic, the coral faces a multitude of other biological threats. Many different invertebrates target the reef, including coral-eating whelks, fireworms and nudibranchs. In the latter case, the corallivores can be hard to spot – they are often small and similar in colour to the coral on which they graze

and sometimes accidentally introduced into a reef aquarium. Many starfish also feed on the coral, stripping away the living polyps as they move across the surface of the colony and leaving a white stripe behind them. Perhaps the most notorious is the crown-of-thorns starfish *(Acanthaster planci)*, which may grow to almost half a metre across. This creature has wreaked havoc in many areas of the world, most notably, perhaps, on the Great Barrier Reef. Like all starfish, it feeds by everting its stomach and dissolving its food – in this case the living polyps

Above: The huge crown-of-thorns starfish (Acanthaster planci) *feeds on corals and is a deadly threat to many reefs across the world, including the Great Barrier Reef.*

– with digestive enzymes. An outbreak of crown-of-thorns starfish presents a serious problem for reef communities, as in high densities they can kill even mature, well-established coral colonies. They do have enemies, including the giant triton (a snail), but until the exact cause of the recent population explosions of this starfish is established, the outlook is bleak for many reefs.

Browsing on the reef

The limestone reef is full of holes, cracks and crannies that hide tasty morsels, such as sponges, shrimps and polychaete worms. Coral polyps are also nutritious, but as they are concealed within their limestone refuge during the day, many fish find them difficult to reach. Nonetheless, certain fish specialise in these apparently well-protected food sources, including members of the butterflyfish and angelfish families.

Below: The extended jaws of the longnose butterflyfish (Forcipiger flavissimus) *enable it to prey on animals hidden deep in the reef.*

Q: *How are the fish adapted to their diet?*

A: Fish that feed on sessile (non-moving) invertebrates such as sponges and corals share the same kind of body plan as the grazing herbivores. Again, deep bodies are ideal for precise manoeuvring, supported by strong pectoral fins that provide great swimming control. But the most noticeable thing about fish that eat coral, or probe into the reef to extract sponges, worms and small crustaceans, is the snout. The extreme example is the longnose butterflyfish (*Forcipiger* spp.), which probes deep into the reef to reach prey that no other fish can.

The shorter snout of the banded butterflyfish (*Chaetodon striatus*) enables it to tackle a wider range of prey, including worms, corals and the occasional crustacean. Within their narrow jaws, most butterflyfish have rows of short, bristlelike teeth with which they can firmly grip their prey as they extract it from its refuge. Polyp-eating specialists such as Meyer's butterflyfish (*Chaetodon meyeri*), and sponge-eating fish such as the regal angelfish (*Pygoplites diacanthus*) have shorter snouts, as they do not need to reach as far into the reef.

Q: *How easy is it for these fish to satisfy their nutritional requirements?*

A: One problem for animals that feed on small prey is that they must spend a great deal of time foraging. Butterflyfish and angelfish are diurnal animals

Chaetodon striatus

Above: The banded butterflyfish has a broad diet and sometimes even cleans parasites from the flanks of other fish.

that gather their food in the 12 hours of the tropical day. Hunger sometimes drives them to continue feeding at night, when there is sufficient light to do so around the time of the full moon, although the increased numbers of fish predators at night makes this a risky strategy. Both families expend huge amounts of energy in their foraging. A study on their feeding rates in the Red Sea showed that the same butterflyfish bit at the surface of the coral, on average, every five seconds throughout the day. By contrast, angelfish were much more relaxed, but even they bit at the reef at about 15-second intervals. Both species feed more

actively in the Red Sea summer, when warm water and the need to fuel breeding efforts lead them to forage more than twice as actively as in winter and spring.

Q: How does the diet of these fish affect their prey populations?

A: Predation is an extremely important force in promoting the highly diverse communities on the reef. Without it, some species would rapidly overcome all their competitors, outgrowing them or taking up all the available space within their habitats. An experiment that involved excluding invertebrate-eating fish from sections of reef using cages, showed that the number of different invertebrate species quickly declined as just a few took over. Predation by angelfish on certain sponges and sea squirts, for example, is known to boost the populations of poorer competitors, such as bryozoans. By the same token, corallivorous fishes prevent certain species of aggressive corals from taking over and allow their competitors to persist, again boosting biodiversity on the reef.

Left: The pipefish (Corythoichthys spp.) examines depressions and holes in the coral for invertebrates.

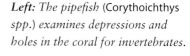

A crunchy lunch

Coral reefs teem with invertebrates – a vital food resource for plenty of different fish. However, prey invertebrates have an impressive array of defences. Perhaps the most common is a tough shell, or carapace, to protect their vulnerable bodies, as seen in crabs, shrimps, urchins, clams and snails. Finding these animals does not often present much of a problem, but any fish that wants to gain access to a juicy meal must first work out how to get past the hard shell.

Below: The redbreasted Maori wrasse (Cheilinus fasciatus) *crushes tough prey, using powerful jaws and plates of pharyngeal teeth.*

Q: What kinds of fish eat these invertebrates?

A: Plenty of fish, ranging from groupers to wrasses and from triggerfish to pufferfish, are equipped to a greater or lesser extent to tackle hard-shelled prey. Crustaceans, such as crabs, shrimps and amphipods, are especially important prey for reef fishes. Molluscs, too, form a major part of fishes' diets in the wild, especially for fish such as goatfish that forage for prey buried in the sandy substrate around reefs.

Q: How do they get through the shell?

A: There are two main ways of getting at the tasty flesh of a shelled animal. One is to bite through the carapace, as pufferfish do. The other is for a fish to crush the prey inside its mouth, using powerful pharyngeal teeth set in the throat. This is the method used by wrasses. Biting is especially useful for tackling prey too large to fit in the mouth. Puffers and porcupinefish have teeth which, like those of parrotfish, are fused into a beak. Iron deposits in the teeth themselves add strength to their impressive bite. Crushers select prey that they can first get into their mouth, so that the pharyngeal teeth can be brought to bear. In both groups, the jaws are powered by extremely strong muscles; those of the redbreast wrasse are something like 500

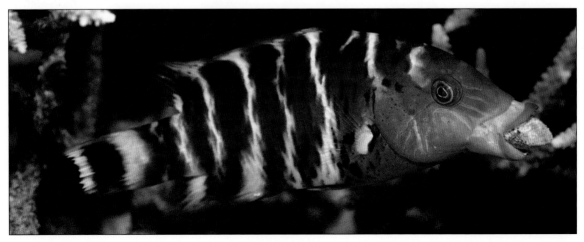

Overcoming tricky prey

*Many prey animals have defences that tax their predators
to the limits, but few can outwit the intelligent triggerfish.*

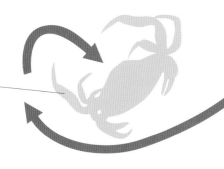

*Nipping
at the
undefended
hind legs
slows
down the
crab.*

*Blowing a jet of water turns the
crab on its back, exposing its
vulnerable undersides to attack.*

times stronger than those of fish that graze on soft foods, allowing the fish to crunch just about any prey. As well as these impressive crushing teeth, many wrasse have spiky teeth protruding beyond their jaws with which they prise their prey from holdfasts.

Q: *What other strategies do fish have for dealing with well-defended prey?*

A: Crabs are well defended, not only by their tough exoskeleton, but also by their claws. Tackling such feisty prey requires a strategy, especially when prey and predator are fairly well matched in size. Young queen triggerfish have two methods of attacking crabs: the first exploits the fact that the crab is inflexible and cannot defend all parts of

its body, so if the crab is caught in the open, the trigger can bite at its hind legs or towards the back of its carapace. The trigger can also blow jets of water to unbalance the crab – once it is on its back, the crab is beaten. Triggerfish – amongst the most intelligent of all fish – also have strategies for dealing with the spines of sea urchins. Again, they may use jets of water to upend the urchins, but some populations are known to carry the urchin to the top of the water column where it is released, allowing the fish to bite at the softer underparts as the urchin drifts towards the bottom.

*Below: Wrasses, such as this moon
wrasse, crunch small, shelled
invertebrates and do a valuable
job in keeping these animals under
control.*

Not just filter feeders

It is not only fish that prey on reef invertebrates, nor do these invertebrates live a life of grazing and filter feeding; there are some fearsome predators amongst the invertebrates. These hunters have adopted some innovative strategies to get past the sometimes quite considerable defences of their fellow inverts, and some of these hunters are capable of taking on and subduing adult fish.

Q: *How do invertebrates get past tough physical defences, such as shells?*

A: Some starfish make their living by feeding on molluscs. The major barrier between them and a meal is their prey's shell, but this can be overcome if the right tactics are used. Starfish move using thousands of tube feet and these can be pressed into service for opening up a bivalve. Having located its bivalve prey, the starfish envelopes it and gradually exerts intense pressure in an attempt to gain access, applying an incredible force at the bivalve's hinge. Then it is a straightforward battle between the muscles of

Above: Octopuses are highly intelligent predators of other invertebrates. Once it has engulfed its prey, the octopus can deliver a killing bite with its powerful beak.

the protagonists, but few clams can stand up to the starfish. Certainly, any creature less than 10cm long is in real trouble if a starfish gets hold of it. For this reason, clams can move if they see or smell the presence of a starfish in the area. If a shadow passes over their simple eyes,

they take in a shellful of water and then rapidly contract their muscles, forcing a jet of water out of their exhalant siphon and jetting off at high speed. Many octopuses have also faced the problem of shelled prey. Crabs are a favourite food amongst these super-intelligent predators and even large, aggressive crabs stand little chance when caught in the open by an octopus. The octopus – which is itself a mollusc, a relative of clams and sea slugs – simply wraps up the victim in its tentacles and brings its powerful central beak to bear on the crab's carapace.

Q: How do invertebrates eat prey that is larger than themselves?

A: A problem for invertebrates such as shrimps is that their prey is often considerably larger than they are. One example is the harlequin shrimp, which takes on comparatively huge starfish as its prey. The first problem facing the shrimp when it comes across a starfish is how to tear its prey away from the substrate. It approaches this by nipping at the echinoderm's tube feet, but a starfish can have thousands of these and often it seems that as fast as the shrimp detaches some of the starfish's tube feet, more fasten on. If the shrimp persists, it may eventually manage to dislodge the starfish. However, better results are achieved with teamwork, and harlequins often approach the problem of such tenacious prey in pairs. Once the shrimp or shrimps have managed to detach the starfish from its hold, the battle is virtually over; the shrimps turn the starfish onto its back and carry it back to their home range, where they can eat it – alive – sometimes over a period of days.

Above: Harlequin shrimps use teamwork to overcome starfish. Having flipped over the echinoderm, they can feed on its tube feet.

Audacious invertebrates

The 'kill-or-be-killed' world of invertebrate hunters and their victims is like something from a science fiction novel, but as is often the case, truth is stranger than fiction. Some of the most remarkable predators can be found amongst these predatory reef invertebrates.

Left: Cone shells, such as Conus textile, are fearsome and deadly predators. Their extremely toxic venom rapidly paralyses and kills their prey.

Q: *How do predators overcome chemical defences?*

A: Potentially vulnerable animals on the reef often use powerful defences to discourage their predators. However, the stinging tentacles of anemones are not always enough to discourage predatory nudibranchs. Having found their prey by following trails of chemical cues, the nudibranch approaches very carefully, avoiding touching the anemone and thereby triggering its defence response, which is to withdraw into itself. The nudibranch raises itself high above the unsuspecting anemone, keeping itself clear of the stinging tentacles. Finally, when it is above the centre of the anemone, the nudibranch everts its mouthparts and plunges

Killer cones

The cone shell's harpoon is similar to a bee's sting: both have barbs to hold them in their victim's flesh while venom is pumped into the wound.

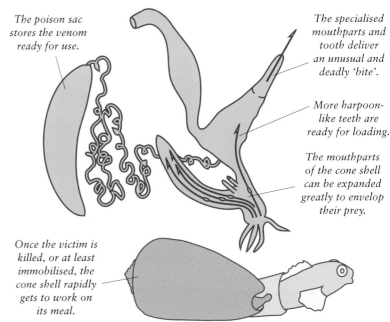

The poison sac stores the venom ready for use.

The specialised mouthparts and tooth deliver an unusual and deadly 'bite'.

More harpoon-like teeth are ready for loading.

The mouthparts of the cone shell can be expanded greatly to envelop their prey.

Once the victim is killed, or at least immobilised, the cone shell rapidly gets to work on its meal.

downwards, deep into its prey. Although the anemone responds by withdrawing its tentacles, it is too late to save itself – within its body, the nudibranch is already feeding. The stinging cells of the anemone are recycled by the nudibranchs that eat them and stored underneath their own skin, where they continue to provide protection.

Q: Do any invertebrates prey on fish?

A: Fish make excellent prey for invertebrates, but they are extremely elusive and difficult to subdue. This is why fish-eating marine snakes have far more potent venom than their land cousins; marine snakes are under pressure to kill their prey quickly because a wounded fish can swim far out of range in just a few seconds. The potency of marine snakes is matched by that of some cone shells. These animals can reach a considerable size – up to 20cm – but like most snails, are extremely slow moving. To capture fish, they rely on a harpoonlike mechanism to carry deadly venom into their victim's tissues and paralyse them, in some cases almost instantly. Their venom is so powerful that some cone shells can cause serious injury to, or even kill, humans.

The 'cigarette snail' is so-called because an attack by this animal is thought to leave little time for anything other than a final smoke!

Q: What is the most dramatic invertebrate predator?

A: The ultra-versatile cephalopods (octopus, squid, etc.) are remarkably successful hunters, but in terms of their incredible weaponry, the mantis shrimps are hard to beat. They can mobilise their folded claws to strike their prey amazingly quickly, generating speeds approaching those of a bullet. In fact, the acceleration is so fast that it causes a cavitation bubble to form in the water, so that the victim is hit not only with the claw, but also with the even greater shock of the bubble. Some species of these shrimps spear their prey, impaling soft-bodied animals such as fish with spiny, barbed appendages. Other species smash shelled quarry using a more rounded clublike claw and then dismember their victim with a sharper, more versatile claw.

Below: Mantis shrimps are amongst the most dangerous reef predators, employing smash-and-grab tactics to overcome large and often armoured prey.

Feeding – invertebrate style

By far the majority of individual marine invertebrates on the coral reef feed on microscopic prey borne on the ocean currents, sifting it from the water with a variety of net- and meshlike body parts. These filter-feeding animals are usually sessile, or at the least slow moving, so they rely on their food to come to them, rather than the other way around.

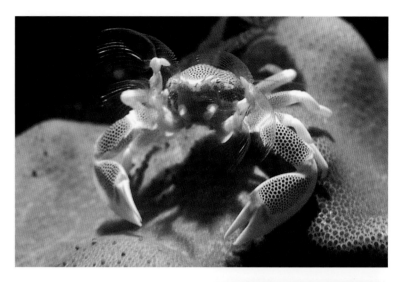

Q: *Which invertebrates are filter feeders?*

A: As well as the coral polyps (see page 72), animals such as tubeworms, basket stars, clams, sponges and even some kinds of crabs feed by filtering plankton from the water as it moves past them. Most of these animals feed at night, thereby avoiding the risk of exposing vulnerable body parts during the day, when so many fish predators are active. By concentrating their foraging activity into the night-time period, filter feeders can also benefit from the migration of unimaginable numbers of zooplankton as they rise to the surface waters at night to feed on microscopic plants.

Above: Many animals, such as Petrolisthes maculatus, *have developed meshed limbs for gathering particles in the water.*

Right: Tubeworms collect food in specialised branched appendages. These particles can then be fed directly into the mouth.

Q: *How do filter feeders capture their prey?*

A: A prerequisite for a filter feeder is to be situated in at least some water current, so that it can feed on the tiny animals that flow past it as if on a conveyor belt. After this, there are a few different strategies. Filter-feeding

crabs have claws like mesh baskets that they sweep through the water. Anything they catch is then directed towards the mouth. Other animals, such as sea squirts and sponges, have millions of tiny hairs, known as cilia, which beat in waves and increase the flow of water – and plankton – into them. This food is either directed straight into the mouth or caught in a mucus-lined trap that catches all the particles in the water before the animal ingests them, like fly paper. The idea of a sticky trap is also used by sea cucumbers, which extend branched and slightly sticky tentacles into the current to capture their food. However, not all sea cucumbers feed like this; some push their feeding tentacles out across the substrate to feed on organic particles that sink out of the water column. Bivalves also feed by filtering the water they draw into themselves to breathe. Like corals, giant clams have symbiotic algae living in the exposed portion of their mantle, which also supply them with food. Some sponge species enter the same relationship with algae to help them satisfy all their nutritional requirements.

Q: How do polyps and anemones deal with larger prey?

A: Plankton is a term that describes a huge variety of small, unrelated animals and plants. They vary enormously in size; some zooplankton may be hundreds of times larger than phytoplankton. Larger members of the plankton are more nutritious, but also more mobile and likely to resist capture by basic mechanical means. Such prey may need to be subdued, and anemones and their relatives achieve this using nematocysts (see page 73). When triggered, these cells release tiny harpoonlike structures that are attached to the anemone or polyp by threads. They drive into the flesh of the prey, spinning anticlockwise to go deeper and delivering toxins to paralyse.

Right: Pseudocolochirus axiologus, *a sea apple, feeds on particles suspended in the water, using the fernlike appendages on its head.*

Fish food from the water

Tides and ocean currents deliver a continuous supply of microscopic plants and animals past coral reefs. This abundance of food supports a huge number of sea creatures, from the corals all the way up to enormous animals such as manta rays and the biggest of them all, the whale shark. A large number of more normally sized fishes also feed on the plankton, facing into the currents above the reef to harvest their needs from the mass of tiny copepods, cladocerans and invertebrate larvae transported across the reef by water currents.

Q: What kinds of fish feed on plankton?

A: Just about all tropical marine fishes undergo a planktonic stage early in their development, where they live as larvae amongst the plankton. Once settled on the reef, plenty of species diversify into different diets, but equally, a large number continue with their planktivorous diet. Almost all major families have planktivorous members; there are plenty of examples amongst the damselfish, basslets and butterflyfish that

feed during the day and amongst nocturnal feeders, such as squirrelfish and cardinalfish.

Q: How are they adapted to their diet?

A: Diurnal planktivores feed on relatively small members of the zooplankton, such as copepods. These prey animals are usually transparent, all are usually smaller

than 3mm and many measure less than 1mm. Spotting them requires excellent eyesight – one characteristic of the fishes that feed on them. The fish also tend to have small mouths and toothless jaws, with tightly packed gill rakers to prevent the escape of captured prey. They have forked tails and, usually, streamlined bodies that allow them to spend long periods

facing into the currents as they feed. These features also help the fish to make a fast getaway if danger threatens. Nocturnal planktivores are very different in appearance; their huge eyes allow them to see their prey in the dark and their mouths are equally large. One reason for this

Below: The squarespot anthias (Pseudanthias pleurotaenia) *lives in large groups along the reef edge, where it can feed on zooplankton carried in the currents.*

latter feature is the size of their prey, which is considerably larger than that of diurnal fish – almost always greater than 2mm – and includes bigger animals, such as mysid shrimps.

Q: *How do they feed on the plankton?*

A: Diurnal planktivores face into the current, especially on the outer walls of reefs, picking at their food as it drifts past. The further away the fish venture

from the protection of the reef, the more food they can find, but this comes at the cost of a much greater risk of attack from patrolling predatory fish. For this reason, diurnal planktivores tend to feed in groups for safety, and the aggregations are structured by size – the larger, faster-swimming fish can afford to take more risks and feed furthest away from the reef. Sometimes these fish switch from their regular diet to exploit new types of food: when corals, or even large fish such as parrotfish spawn, sizeable groups of planktivores gather downstream to feast. The nocturnal planktivores feed in a very different way. As they leave their huge resting aggregations, they split up into small, loose groups or even go solo, spreading across the reef to gather their superabundant prey.

Soup at sea

Plankton is a catch-all term covering a huge variety of microscopic plants (phytoplankton) and animals (zooplankton). At night, when plankton is at its most dense in the surface waters, a torch beam will attract swarms of these tiny creatures.

Breakfast on the seabed

The sandy plains and seagrass beds that exist in coral lagoons and in the spaces between large coral heads are home to a variety of invertebrates, including molluscs, worms and shrimps. Some of these animals seek shelter by hiding beneath the sand at certain times throughout the day, away from the attentions of their predators. But as far as some fish are concerned, out of sight is not necessarily out of mind. Quite a few fish species, including goatfish, cowfish and many wrasse, use some ingenious tactics to seek out hidden prey.

Q: How does the goatfish find its prey?

A: Goatfish use a pair of barbels on the chin to dig into the sandy substrate in pursuit of buried prey. The barbels themselves are covered with chemosensory cells, so that as the fish sifts through the sand, it is able to taste that which it cannot see. Foraging goatfish kick up large clouds of fine sand as they root around on the seabed and this attracts a crowd of other fish, which hang around in the hope of picking up a free meal in the shape of a disturbed creature from below.

Q: What other kinds of fish forage in the lagoons?

A: Seahorses are usually found amongst seagrass beds in lagoons, holding onto the vegetation with their prehensile tails and snapping at passing invertebrates in the water column. The bizarrely shaped cowfishes also occupy the calmer waters of the lagoon. Like their relatives, the puffers and the triggers, they use the remarkable technique of blowing jets of water at the substrate to uncover buried benthic invertebrates. Snake eels lie buried in the sand itself, with only the tip of their snout showing. In this position they can keep a lookout for any prey that crawls or swims too close. If the prey comes within range, the eel explodes from its hiding place and captures its victim before it can react. Lizardfish, too, can be found on these sandy plains and hunt in a similar way to the snake eels, although they do not burrow into the sand. Instead, they rely on patience and camouflage to conceal them from their fish and invertebrate prey.

Below: Coral lagoons are a vital nursery for small fishes and invertebrates. Many of the weaker swimmers, such as seahorses and cowfish, also make their home here.

Q: How else can fish uncover hidden prey on the seabed?

A: Although the remarkable jet-blowing tactics used by the puffers and their relatives to uncover hidden, buried prey probably takes the prize for ingenuity, there are other ways of reaching prey beneath the sand. One method involves taking in a large mouthful of sand and sifting through it, spitting out the sand or ejecting it through the gills and retaining the animals that were sheltered within it. This approach is taken by hogfish, amongst others. Wrasse are extremely active foragers and will make great efforts to secure a meal, including moving or upturning stones on the seabed to expose the selection box beneath.

The hunters

It's dog eat dog – or fish eat fish – on the reef. Predation by larger fish is a fact of life for members of the coral reef community, and this danger plays a large part in shaping many aspects of life there. Fish predators come in all shapes and sizes and include moray eels, jacks, groupers, frogfish, scorpionfish and trumpetfish. Some of these predators use stealth or camouflage to approach close enough to launch a strike on their fish prey. Others prefer out-and-out pace, using their superior swimming speeds to overtake and capture their quarry.

Q: *How do predators operate on the reef?*

A: The most important part of a predator's strategy is to get close to its prey. Close-range attacks, combined with the element of surprise, offer the best chance of success. Even so, it is estimated that far fewer than half of all attacks are successful. Prey fish have evolved over millions of years to be able to respond extremely quickly to

Below: Piscivorous predators, such as this lyretail grouper, often lurk under overhanging ledges and in crevices waiting for smaller fish to venture too close.

any sudden disturbance. They are capable of incredible turns of speed in the milliseconds following the detection of a predator; if the hunter fails to take its prey straightaway its chances of a meal are minimal.

Q: *How are predators adapted for their diet?*

A: One thing that most fish predators have in common is a large mouth, which can be opened rapidly to create considerable suction when the predator strikes. This suction draws the prey into the mouth at the last moment. In addition, predators usually have sharp, peglike teeth that point inwards; once caught in these teeth, there is little possibility of escape. Finally, fish predators usually have a large throat, allowing many of them to attack fish that are barely any smaller than themselves.

Q: *What tactics do the hunters use?*

A: Open-water predators, such as jacks, use speed to overtake and then capture their prey, sometimes working in teams

The grouper's large mouth is typical of a predatory fish – many can tackle prey that are over half their size.

to corral their prey into tight groups or up against obstacles that block their escape. But most of the predators that actually live on the reef use some kind of stealth tactic. This might take the shape of camouflage, as used by ambush predators such as the scorpionfish and lizardfish. Scorpionfish and frogfish sometimes have small lures, formed by extensions of their dorsal fin, to entice smaller fish to inspect what looks like a tasty morsel. The curiosity that causes these fish to approach usually costs them their lives. Another remarkable strategy is that of fish such as groupers and lionfish, which mingle – apparently innocently – with groups of prey fish until these lose their wariness of the predator and approach too closely, with fatal consequences. Or they might stalk their prey, as trumpetfish and smaller jacks do. Trumpetfish are the absolute masters of this. They may conceal themselves within a shoal of harmless fish in order to get closer, or hide behind another fish, even to the extent of taking on its colour, in order to try to convince their quarry that they are not there. Other fish, especially sharks and moray eels, hunt under cover of darkness, looking for unwary or badly concealed resting fish.

Above: The clearfin lionfish (Pterois radiata) is a master of stealth, patiently edging towards its prey before launching a strike.

Below: Streamlined open-water predators, such as blue-spotted jacks, patrol just off the reef, ruthlessly hunting down prey fish.

Chapter 5
Dodging predators

The coral reef is a dangerous place for all its inhabitants; most animals live in close proximity to a host of dangers and different kinds of predators. Their survival depends on their defences and their ability to break the predation cycle.

For reef fish, self-preservation tactics range from keeping alert and learning the lay of the land to anatomical adaptations. Reef animals show an incredible array of anti-predator defences, including spines, agility, camouflage, self-inflation, poisonousness and mimicry.

Q: How have fish got better at fighting back?

A: Only fish that are successful in dodging predators get the chance to breed and pass on their genes. Those characteristics that enabled the parent fish to survive are then passed on through the genes to their offspring and so the process of evolution advances in tiny incremental steps. But while successive generations of prey fish become fractionally better able to avoid their predators, the predators respond in kind, producing an 'arms race' of adaptation and counter-adaptation. The astonishing adaptations that reef fish show are the results of this process, spanning millions of years and countless generations of fishes.

Above: The long, bony spines of this sea urchin protect it from the casual interest of many potential predators and provide a place for small and vulnerable fishes to dart into whenever they feel threatened.

Q: How do fish break the predation cycle?

A: Fishes' defences against predation can kick in at any stage of the so-called predation cycle. Some try to avoid detection by predators in the first place using camouflage or by hiding. Others try to deter predator attack by bluff, by being poisonous or through their behaviour. Most fish remain highly alert in the presence of predators, ready to dart away at speed. And if the worst comes to the worst, others have evolved armour and spines so that a predator is unlikely to be able to devour them. Here, we consider each of these strategies, looking at the diverse ways in which fish attempt to overcome their hunters.

Q: What about predation in the aquarium?

A: If all runs to plan, predation ought not to be a concern for domestic animals – or should it? Although this is true, fish in the home aquarium still display the behaviour and appearance of their wild ancestors – what may be called the 'ghost of predation past'. Clownfish still seek shelter in their home anemone, shrimps still hide amongst the aquarium decor and porcupinefish retain their spiky wardrobe. As more and more marine animals are bred and raised in captivity to supply the aquarium trade, we should expect to see some slight changes in behaviour. For example, in tropical freshwater fish, which have been cultivated for much longer than most tropical marines, domestication produces fish that are bolder than their wild counterparts

Above: Everything about the appearance of the Halimeda ghost pipefish is perfectly in tune with its immediate habitat.

and less likely to take fright. Even so, we should remember that predation has had a huge influence on fish for millions of years and it takes more than a few generations for the ghost of its effect to depart.

How not to be noticed

When predators are at large, it obviously pays to be inconspicuous. One way is to blend into the background in the hope of avoiding detection by a hunter. Camouflage, or crypsis, is widely used on the reef for this purpose. An animal that can successfully blend into its background will live a great deal longer than one that stands out. But one disadvantage of being inconspicuous is that you cannot advertise yourself to potential mates or warn competitors to keep off your patch. Some fishes solve this conundrum by changing colour as they grow. Virtually transparent larvae can adopt dull, camouflaging colours as juveniles before becoming brightly coloured, fully grown adults. Anatomically, animals can try to avoid predators in a variety of ways: they can match the colours of their background, they can disguise their outline or they can pretend to be something else.

Right: Camouflage is important for prey animals and also for predators such as stonefish, which are often not noticed until it is too late.

Q: *Is camouflage a common strategy on the reef?*

A: Plenty of different animals use basic camouflage. Fish that occupy the waters surrounding the reef, but live freely in the water column, are often silvery, which is the most effective livery for open-water survival. Larval reef fishes are mainly transparent, again an adaptation that helps them to stay as invisible as possible to visual hunters. Countershading, where the dorsal surface of the fish is fairly dark in comparison to the pale – even white – colouring of the underside, is also common amongst fishes. It helps the fish to blend in, both against a dark background when seen from above and against the sky when viewed from beneath. But these adaptations are fairly basic compared to the camouflage seen in some reef inhabitants.

Q: Do nocturnal fish bother with camouflage?

A: At night, complex camouflage is less important because of the restricted light levels. One effective strategy in these conditions is to have an almost uniformly reddish body, as seen in nocturnal plankton-feeders, such as squirrelfish. This may seem strange, but because red light is absorbed rapidly by water, anything red is perceived as being a dark and neutral colour. As anyone who has ever cut themselves while diving will know, the blood from the cut appears to be a dark green!

Q: What about the bright colours of diurnal fishes?

A: It has long been thought that the dazzling colours of reef fish are a real disadvantage when it comes to avoiding predators. The vivid blues, yellows and reds advertise effectively to rivals and to mates, but the by-product is that they act as a 'come and get me' sign to visual hunters. Or so it was thought. New research suggests that bright colours may work both as signals and as camouflage. To understand why, we need to take a predator's eye view, because the visual abilities of fish and of humans

Left: Camouflage only works effectively when it is in tune with the background environment. This blenny puts itself at risk by failing to match up.

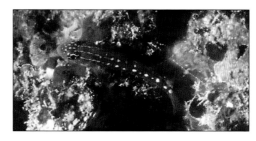

Left: The same fish retreats to its more accustomed home and becomes far less conspicuous. Its mottled pattern and colours blend in perfectly.

are different. When researchers used imaging techniques to adopt a predator's perspective, it became clear that although the bright colour patterns of many small reef fishes are extremely conspicuous close up, at a distance of just a few metres these patterns function amazingly well at camouflaging the animals. This is because patterns such as stripes and spots blur together against the complex visual

background of the reef. Moreover, blue and yellow – commonly seen in reef fish – provide very good camouflage against both the reef and the open water when seen from a few metres away and from a predator's perspective.

Below: Many small fishes on the reef, such as this clingfish, are extremely specific in their choice of habitat and this is reflected in the precision of their colour patterns.

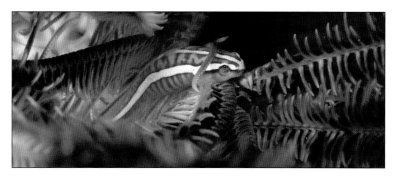

Chameleons of the sea

Small animals on the reef are in constant danger of ending up as a snack for the ever-hungry predators patrolling the area. This fact of life has driven the evolution of some remarkable adaptations, not least those used by reef animals to blend into their background. For camouflage to be most effective, animals must not only match their colour to the surrounding habitat, but also manage to break up the outline and contours of their body.

Q: *How common is camouflage amongst reef animals?*

A: In the predator-rich world of the coral reef, it pays to keep a low profile and camouflage is an extremely common strategy. It is especially frequent among animals closely associated with a particular microhabitat within the reef. There are many examples of gobies that are exquisitely matched to their habitat, particularly coral gobies. Invertebrates, too, use camouflage extensively. The candy crab, for example, is perfectly adapted to blend in against the soft coral amongst which it lives.

Q: *What is contour elimination?*

A: Many fish predators operate by forming a search image; their mind focuses on finding fish-shaped objects. Prey animals work in the same way when they are keeping an eye out for an approaching predator. Contour elimination, as the term suggests, works by breaking up this outline and is a key part of blending into the background. The decorator crab is covered in tiny hairs that work almost like Velcro. The crab covers itself in pieces of debris and aquatic bric-a-brac that it comes across until ultimately it ceases to look like a crab at all. It has also been suggested that stripes, especially vertical stripes such as those of Moorish idols, are also highly effective in breaking up an

Left: Texture and the ability to keep still are effective camouflage. This crab is likely to be overlooked by all but the most persistent predators, unless it moves.

known as adaptive camouflage. Furthermore, many seahorses are able to match not only the colour of their habitat, but also its texture. They display amazing patterns of contour elimination as well; the incredible leafy sea dragon *(Phycodurus eques)* is a good example of this. The related pygmy seahorses *(Hippocampus bargibanti)* live amongst soft corals and are almost impossible to detect, even at close range, so well do they match their surroundings. If transferred to a new sea fan, they rapidly take on both the colour and texture of their new host.

Above: The outline of the tasselled filefish is broken up by growths of skin, making the fish far less conspicuous in its natural habitat.

animal's outline. Predators, such as scorpionfishes and frogfishes, also use contour elimination to prevent their prey detecting and avoiding them. These bottom-living fish often have a ragged fringe around their bodies. When viewed from above, it helps them blend in against the corals. Most highly camouflaged animals, including those that use contour elimination, keep very still for large portions of their day; any movement would counteract the effectiveness of their disguise.

Q: Who are the real marine chameleons?

A: Flatfish, such as plaice and flounder, were once considered the masters of disguise, changing colour to match the substrate on which they lie. However, the real champions are arguably the seahorses. In common with flatfishes, they are able to adapt their coloration to match their surroundings, a quality

Right: It is virtually impossible to see where this pygmy seahorse ends and the coral that it lives amongst begins. Such expert camouflage is usually only adopted by relatively sedentary animals.

Mimicry – an effective defence

Given a choice between tackling an angry moray eel or a small, inoffensive morsel of a fish, there are no prizes for guessing which one a predator is likely to opt for. But if the small fish in question can fool the predator into thinking it is a moray eel, then it is very likely to be left alone. The remarkable coloration and pattern of the comet *(Calloplesiops altivelis)* is thought to mimic whitemouth moray eels. The comet seeks refuge headfirst, so that its flowing fins and startling eyespot remain exposed, looking for all the world like the protruding head of a fearsome moray eel, something that few hunters will willingly tackle. The comet even takes things a step further if threatened and has mastered the art of swimming backwards. When it does so, the appearance is startlingly like that of a moray eel swimming forwards. Mimicry such as this is fairly common on coral reefs. Many harmless organisms mimic more dangerous or poisonous species (known as Batesian mimicry, see also page 109)

and some predators mimic harmless fish to get up close to their prey (known as aggressive mimicry).

Q: *Can you always believe your eyes?*

A: Comets are not the only fish to use eyespots, or ocelli, to confuse predators. Eyespots are a simple but ingenious way of confusing predators. Firstly, the eyespots that fish such as butterflyfish incorporate into their colour patterns are usually larger than their own eyes. This is important, because there is evidence to suggest that predators use the size of their prey's eye to gauge how large they are, especially when they cannot see the whole of their quarry's body. This is particularly

The mimic and its model

The harmless comet resembles a deadly whitemouth moray eel. Most potential predators of the comet back off, rather than take a chance!

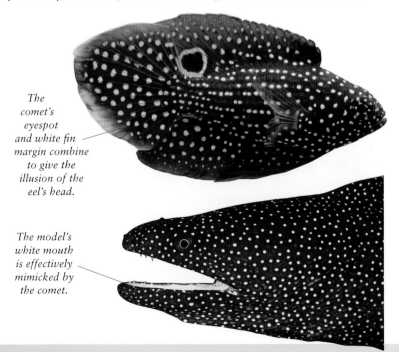

The comet's eyespot and white fin margin combine to give the illusion of the eel's head.

The model's white mouth is effectively mimicked by the comet.

Left: Large, widely spaced eyes confuse and deter predators. Anything approaching the grubfish from above will be startled by this remarkable colour pattern.

opposite direction to that which the predator would expect! Finally, eyespots are also thought to direct attacks away from the head area and towards the less vulnerable tail area.

Q: What is meant by 'deflective coloration'?

A: Any colour pattern that fishes use to redirect a potential attack away from the head and eyes and towards a different part of their body is referred to as deflective coloration. Eyespots fall into this category, but are not the only type. An impressive example is seen in juvenile emperor angelfishes, whose mesmerising concentric bands are thought to achieve the same effect. Interestingly, a number of predators have a similar strategy, using colour patterns to draw prey fish closer, a phenomenon known as directive coloration. Examples include the lures, often shaped like worms, used by some anglerfishes, and the vividly coloured mouthparts of stargazers.

the case in many wrasse species, gurnards and crab eye gobies; the dual eyespots of these fishes may momentarily convince predators into thinking that they have come face to face with a really huge animal! If they can be confused into thinking that the large eyespot belongs to a large fish, they will be less likely to attack. Secondly, the eyespot tends to be located towards the rear of the body, while the real eyes are partially masked by a band of coloration. If and when a predator attacks, its prey will escape in exactly the

Below: The pattern of the juvenile emperor angelfish is now thought to be an aid to protect the most vulnerable areas of the fish's body.

Attacks are directed away from the head towards the tail.

A place to hide

The complex limestone structure of a coral reef provides a huge number of hiding places for prey animals. Unfortunately for them, these hiding places are far from infallible; slender-bodied predators, such as moray eels and whitetip reef sharks, are built for investigating the smallest gaps and crevices in the reef. Whereas some prey fish simply seek safety in numbers as they rest in crowded refuges underneath coral overhangs, other species have adopted remarkable strategies to try to outfox their predators.

Q: Where are the best refuges on the reef?

A: Given that predators are generally larger than their prey, the best refuges are obviously those that are inaccessible to them. The reef provides plenty of bolt-holes and even the most discerning customer can find a good hiding place. Holes in coral are used extensively by fish such as blennies, some of which gain extra protection by making their home inside stinging fire coral. When they take up residence in

a night-time refuge, triggerfish can lock themselves in by clicking their dorsal fin ray into position. And pearlfish actually shelter inside sea cucumbers. This was once thought to be an innocent lodging arrangement, as the fish eats mainly small fish and crustaceans, but more recently it has been suggested that the lodger grazes on its host while hiding within.

Above: The reef offers many refuges for small fish, such as this blenny, protecting them from the attentions of many predators and providing good nest sites.

Q: Where else can fish hide?

A: Quite a few fish use the sandy substrate of the seabed in the lagoons or around the reef as an emergency retreat. Wrasse are particularly adept at slicing into the sand, disappearing with a flick of the tail. The razorfish has perfected the same technique, not only to hide but also to hunt for buried invertebrates and small fish, such as garden eels. Sand tilefish build a rubble pile on the seabed, diving into it if danger threatens. Jawfish build burrows tailored exactly to their own body size for this reason. When they sense a predator they retreat into their designer refuge tail-first and may even close off the top with a pebble.

Q: *How do parrotfish escape the attentions of nocturnal predators?*

A: Nocturnal predators make extensive use of their sense of smell when locating prey. By sleeping in a cocoon, parrotfishes contain their own chemical signature and prevent it from spreading around the local area and potentially to the noses of predators. Each night the fish spends 20 to 30 minutes manufacturing its mucus cocoon. Once secreted, the mucus becomes firmer, acquiring

an almost rubbery texture, and the fish is able to rest within. If a predator does inspect the mucus cocoon, the disturbed parrotfish will shoot out of it, leaving behind the shell, which may serve to distract the hunter just long enough to allow its prey to escape. As well as its anti-predator function, the sac also has anti-bacterial properties that keep the resting fish safe from a host of unpleasant pathogens.

Below: Like many diurnal fish, parrotfish seek shelter within the structures of the reef at nightfall.

Chemical weapons

Slow or sessile animals that live on the reef are under constant investigation by fish, amongst other things, to see whether they might make a meal. A study into the intensity of fish foraging showed that each square metre of exposed coral reef is pecked or bitten by fish over 100,000 times every single day. Faced with this kind of bite barrage, it is perhaps of little surprise that so many reef animals use chemical defences to discourage attacks.

Q: How many reef inverts are actually poisonous?

A: To test this, researchers conducted fish-feeding experiments. The results revealed that every single soft-bodied and slow-moving reef invertebrate was unpalatable to fish. Now, although unpalatable does not mean poisonous, it is a step along that road; given a choice, a fish will avoid eating them. True toxicity, or poisonousness, obviously provides a better defence. The downside is that developing and running a powerful defence comes at the cost of something else. It might

Above: Predators expecting a juicy worm may have a nasty surprise in store – these bearded fireworms are covered in small spiny hairs to discourage attackers.

mean that the animal has to forage more exhaustively or is unable to produce as many eggs. Even so, it is estimated that over half the common, vulnerable, reef invertebrates are actually toxic as adults to fish.

Q: How do invertebrates use chemical defences?

A: Different animals employ different tactics to fit different needs. Sea urchins are at risk of becoming coated in encrusting organisms, so the surface of their shells is covered in tiny pincerlike structures called pedicellariae. In some species, these are modified to add to their arsenal of anti-predator defences. Other species, such as Savigny's sea urchin, augment the forbidding nature of their spines with toxins. Polychaete worms are covered in tiny bristles (polychaete means 'many bristles'), which are poisonous in some species, each bristle having its own venom sac. Like bee stings, these bristles may snap off and lodge in the flesh of an attacker, where they act as an irritant. Sea cucumbers

Left: If disturbed, some species of sea cucumber are able to produce copious amounts of toxic or sticky threads.

Below: Many nudibranchs have bright colours that often serve to advertise that they are poisonous to potential predators.

use a dramatic technique when they are disturbed, apparently almost turning themselves inside-out to eject a white substance. This series of white threads may be sticky in order to gum up predators, or may carry a potent poison called holothurin, which weakens the muscles of the predator. It seems that South Pacific islanders once used this substance for fishing – if added to a lagoon or an isolated pool at low tide it poisoned the fish, allowing them to be harvested. Other species simply borrow or steal the chemical defences of others: nudibranchs recycle the stinging cells of their anemone

prey for their own use, while boxer crabs ingeniously attach an anemone to each claw.

Q: *Which are the most poisonous reef invertebrates?*

A: There are plenty of poisonous invertebrates whose chemical defences, often accidentally triggered, can have serious – even fatal – effects on humans. Many jellyfish are best avoided, but amongst true reef species, cone shells can be very dangerous; around 20% of people 'harpooned' by them die. If touched, fire coral is also extremely unpleasant, though rarely fatal. Despite its small size and retiring nature, the blue-ringed octopus demands respect. Its bite has enough venom to kill over 20 adult humans in minutes and there is no known antidote.

Poisonous fishes

Reef fishes face the same predation pressures as invertebrates, so it is perhaps not surprising that some of them, too, defend themselves with toxins. However, fish have fewer methods of deploying their poisons. In most cases, they inflict them using their fin rays, and for good reason: spiny fin rays are excellent for piercing the skin of a predator's mouth (or an unwary hand), while glands at the base of the fin and grooves in the ray itself shoot a dose of toxin rapidly into their attacker. For the poison to be useful to the fish, it must be fast acting, otherwise by the time it has had any effect on a predator, it will be too late for the victim.

Q: *What makes a reef fish likely to be poisonous?*

A: Coral reef species have a range of defences against predation, but for those species whose lifestyles put them in the firing line toxins can be invaluable. Slow, small and solitary fishes are most at risk from predators, and pufferfish and their relatives are all of these. Their unusual method of swimming means they cannot

Below: Even inoffensive fishes, such as the citron goby, produce chemicals in their skin mucus that are distasteful or even poisonous to predators.

out-swim a predator; most species are small and the distribution of their food means they are often solitary, so they become sitting targets – little wonder they are so deadly poisonous. But puffers are not the only poisonous fish on the reef; species as diverse as the *Plotosus* catfish, the foxface and blue-lined surgeonfish incorporate poison into their defences through venomous spiny fin rays. Lionfish bristle with poisonous fin rays and would make a thoroughly unpleasant mouthful for any predator naïve enough to attack them. Small, coral-dwelling gobies of the *Gobiodon* genus, which would otherwise be prey for many hunters, produce toxic skin secretions. Most predators avoid them, even steering clear of pieces of harmless food that have been experimentally wiped with the mucus of these fish.

Diodon holocanthus has a coating of spines.

Above: The bodies of slow-swimming fish, such as the spiny puffer, are laced with a cocktail of toxic chemicals.

Q: How toxic can coral reef fish get?

A: Fish can be toxic in two ways, either adopting a form of chemical defence against their predators as discussed above, or as a by-product of their diet. Pufferfish and their relatives have some of the most effective chemical defences known amongst all fish. Their bodies are laced with an extremely powerful nerve toxin known as tetrodotoxin, which is over 1,000 times more potent than cyanide. Some species are more poisonous than others, but the most toxic of these produce enough poison to kill 30 people.

Lionfish, scorpionfish and stonefish use chemical defences, too, but of these, only the stonefish is usually likely to be fatal to humans. At the top of the marine food chain are many predatory fish that are poisonous for humans – and potentially other mammals – to eat. The reason for this is ciguatera poisoning. Marine dinoflagellates produce this toxin, which is passed up the food chain. The dinoflagellates are eaten by the herbivores, which in turn are eaten by predators. At each successive step in the food chain, the ciguatera toxin becomes concentrated in the tissues of the fish. In top predators, such as barracuda, the levels of ciguatera in the animal's flesh are so great that humans can become seriously ill if they eat it.

Below: The fin rays of lionfish, such as Dendrochirus biocellatus, *can penetrate the skin and deliver a dose of deadly chemicals.*

Sending a warning

Although chemical defences can provide excellent protection for many reef organisms, there is always a danger that an inquisitive predator might launch an attack before realising its mistake. Although this may have dire consequences for the attacker, the prey animal may also suffer serious injury. Therefore, it pays animals to advertise their toxicity clearly, making sure that predators get the message well before they become too interested.

Q: Do all inedible animals advertise?

A: Whereas the most dangerous animals usually do invest in warning colours, there are many species that, for whatever reason, do not. Marine sponges are soft bodied and highly vulnerable to fishes but those that live amongst high densities of fishes, such as coral reef sponges, are almost always unpalatable to fish. On the whole, sponges do not use bold warning colours to alert their predators, possibly because they are able to regenerate damaged tissue. But even without these warning colours most fish rarely attack them and even avoid eating fragments of sponges. This may be because the sponges also smell bad or because the fish simply learn to avoid them after an early encounter.

Q: What colour patterns do poisonous animals use as warning signals?

A: In biological terminology, using colour patterns to warn potential predators of danger is known as aposematism. Most poisonous animals are aposematic: the deadly blue-ringed octopus uses a subdued, camouflaged colour pattern for most of its life, but when threatened it flashes the vivid blue warning pattern that gives it its common name. Similarly, the devil scorpionfish blends in with its background under normal conditions, but when threatened it produces a display to warn its assailant of its toxic qualities. However, a warning signal is only effective when it can be generally recognised. For this reason, groups of poisonous animals all tend to converge on the same

Below: Sponges are vulnerable to attack from browsing fish, but are seldom a favourite meal – their flesh is suffused with chemicals that make them unpleasant to eat.

Left: Although normally well-camouflaged, this goblinfish will flash its brightly coloured fins to any predator that disturbs it.

– pretending to be dangerous without actually being so – to protect themselves. On the coral reef, predators avoid the valentine pufferfish and with good reason – it is extremely poisonous. But the blacksaddle filefish (*Paraluteres prionurus*), a completely harmless species, gains protection simply by looking like a valentine pufferfish. However, predators are not stupid; this bluffing strategy only works when there are comparatively few mimicking cheats relative to the number of real poisonous species, otherwise the predators would quickly learn and start to attack.

kinds of signal; for example, many stinging insects, such as bees and wasps, use the combination of yellow and black to give advance warning. The same happens on the reef, where different nudibranch species all adopt the same livery to consolidate the message to any potential predators, a phenomenon known as Mullerian mimicry.

hijacked by perfectly harmless animals that merely pretend to be poisonous. For example, hoverflies have exactly the same colour pattern as wasps but are completely inoffensive; this is known as Batesian mimicry. In effect, the harmless creatures use the wasps' colour pattern

Pretending to be poisonous

Q: Are warning colours mimicked by other reef animals?

A: When large groups of poisonous animals all use the same warning colours to signal that they are poisonous and should not be interfered with, it sends a strong message to their potential predators. But, rather sneakily, the message can be

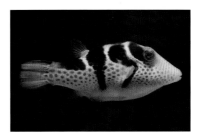

Above: Reef predators recognise Canthigaster valentini *and avoid its potent chemical defences.*

Above: Paraluteres prionurus *is harmless, but is protected by its similarity to* Canthigaster valentini.

Fleeing from danger

Sometimes it can be easy to forget that, despite the ingenious defences used by fish to keep one step ahead of their predators, the one thing that can mean the difference between life and death is a real turn of speed when attacked. Most tropical marine fishes live in close proximity to the reef and are able to dart very rapidly to the safety it provides.

Fins vary between species but most use their tail fin for propulsion, especially for rapid acceleration.

Fishes' bodies are packed with muscle. In most species, the bulk of this is fast-twitch white muscle, which can be used for fast burst swimming to escape danger.

Q: *What gives prey fish their speed?*

A: Fishes' bodies are packages of extremely lean swimming muscle, accounting for up to 80% of the fish's overall weight. In simple terms, this muscle can be divided into two distinct types, distinguishable by their colour. White muscle is used to provide explosive power of the kind used by human sprinters and weightlifters. Red muscle is very well supplied by the blood, as its colour suggests, and is rich in oxygen. It provides steady, long-term power and is used by the animal as it cruises along.

By contrast, white muscle is comparatively poorly supplied by the animal's circulating blood, hence its colour. Although it provides a great deal of power over short distances, enabling the fish to accelerate to safety when danger threatens, white muscle fatigues quickly and few fish can maintain escape speeds for more than a minute. As a result, fish seldom stray so far from their preferred hidey-holes that they cannot dash back when a predator appears. When reef fish are moved into a new habitat, such as an aquarium, they often respond by appearing extremely nervous for the first day or two. This is because they have yet to learn the layout of their local habitat. Gradually, as they are able to assess where refuge is to be found, they calm down noticeably.

Q: *How can fish maximise their chances of making it to safety?*

A: Although reef systems can be huge, most fish remain within relatively small areas, either within their own territory or in a limited home range. In each case, fish are usually excellent at memorising the location of all possible bolt-holes; if a predator attacks, it makes sense to know where to find safety in a hurry. The larger the fish, the more risks it can take. Larger fish have fewer predators and can swim faster than their smaller cousins. Planktivorous reef fishes gather into large aggregations during the day, but these groups are assorted by size: larger fishes are confident enough to stray further from the safety of the reef, while smaller individuals remain close to their shelters.

Q: *How can fish make sure that they spot a predator early?*

A: Reef fish are highly attuned to the behaviour of the other fish in their habitat. If one individual spots an approaching predator and darts for cover, the others will usually respond by following suit. In this way, the danger message is passed rapidly right across all the fish communities on the reef. Although each fish acts as an individual, it benefits from the many eyes that keep a lookout for approaching trouble.

Below: On a coral reef, it makes sense to keep close to a place of safety. Stands of coral make an excellent refuge for chromis shoals.

The chase is on!

When a predator launches an attack, it is time for prey animals to get out of the way with all speed. Of course, anywhere will do to start off with, so long as it is away from danger. However, if the prey animal is cut off from safety, then its life really is in peril. For this reason, reef animals of all types seldom venture too far from their refuge in case they need to beat a hasty retreat.

Q: *How do mobile invertebrates escape when a predator approaches?*

A: Invertebrates use a variety of tactics to accelerate out of harm's way. Many involve a form of jet propulsion, or incredibly fast muscular contractions, to power themselves beyond a predator's deadly intentions. These high-speed manoeuvres not only serve to surprise a hunter; ideally, they should also take the prey animal out of sight and give it a chance to hide while the predator is still wondering what happened. Clams use jet propulsion to shoot out of trouble when disturbed (see

page 82). Their relatives, the octopuses, also use a kind of jet propulsion to escape trouble; many species also leave a decoy cloud of ink behind as they shoot off. Several of the prawns, too, can suddenly disappear from a predator's field of view with a sudden flick of their tail. When attacked by starfish, whelks turn into miniature bucking broncos – rocking furiously in an attempt to dislodge their assailant.

Jetting to safety

When they detect a predator, some species of clam take sudden evasive action and jet to safety.

Q: *What happens if a prey fish is caught in the open?*

A: When this happens and the route to safety is cut off, the odds shift heavily in favour of the predator. But the game is not quite up yet; prey fish still have a few tricks up their sleeves! This is why most predators launch ambushes from hiding places or surprise their prey by

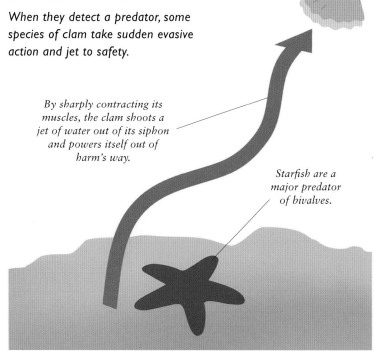

By sharply contracting its muscles, the clam shoots a jet of water out of its siphon and powers itself out of harm's way.

Starfish are a major predator of bivalves.

Out of harm's way

Prey fish isolated from their shoal or away from a hiding place have few options left to them. Erratic swimming – 'skittering' – can sometimes succeed but the prey rapidly reach exhaustion. A different tactic is sometimes called for.

In desperation, prey fish sometimes retreat behind the predator. Although this can only be a temporary measure, it can buy time to recover strength.

attacking them from any blind spot, such as from below when they spot the silhouette of their quarry against the bright surface waters and sky. Fish under attack often adopt a swimming behaviour known as 'skittering'. This refers to the way they dart about rapidly, and apparently haphazardly, turning sharply in different directions. Skittering makes it hard for predators to predict their quarry's next move and ultimately to catch it. As predators are usually larger than their prey and therefore faster swimmers, it would make little sense for an escaping prey fish to dash in a straight line – the predator would simply overtake and capture it. But the size of the predator also makes it less manoeuvrable and the prey exploit this factor with their

sharp banks and turns. However, fish can only play this game for so long – skittering quickly exhausts them – so for safety they must quickly find a hiding place. Sometimes skittering succeeds in

shaking off a predator, but faced with a really persistent hunter, the prey fish may double back and fall in behind the predator, accepting this rather dubious and possibly short-lived haven.

Looming out of the depths

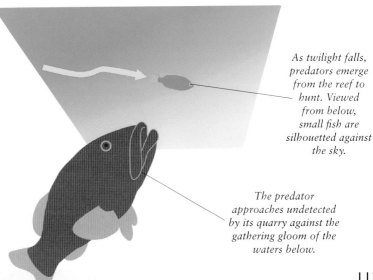

As twilight falls, predators emerge from the reef to hunt. Viewed from below, small fish are silhouetted against the sky.

The predator approaches undetected by its quarry against the gathering gloom of the waters below.

113

A real mouthful

If all else fails – if a predator cannot be discouraged by poisons or be confounded by a dash to safety – then tough, armoured skin or spines may keep it at bay.

Q: How does a fish's morphology relate to the risks that it faces?

A: Most predators of reef fishes, such as groupers, lizardfish and trumpetfish, are gape-limited. This means they can only take prey that they can subdue and fit into their mouths in one go; anything larger than their gape is likely to be passed over in favour of smaller prey. As fish mature and increase in size, the number of predatory species that can handle them steadily reduces. Not all fish are equal in this respect. A goby and a butterflyfish of the same body length present very different problems for a predator, the disk-shaped butterflyfish being much

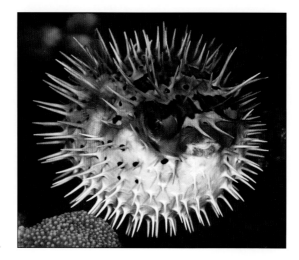

Left: The sudden feat of expansion performed by the spiny puffer (Diodon holocanthus) *not only startles its predators, but also makes it almost impossible to eat.*

more difficult to engulf. This is one reason why reef fishes that live in the water column, and which are therefore more vulnerable to attack, usually have deeper bodies than, say, gobies that live on the substrate.

Q: How do spines help against predatory fish?

A: Growing too large to be a meal for a predator is a slow process. For this reason, many

small fishes develop spines. These work by simply and effectively increasing the size of the prey fish, making them too large for the mouths of their smallest and most numerous predators. Larval reef fishes often have the largest, most elaborate spines. Although these are usually lost during metamorphosis and settlement on the reef, they help to neutralise the threat of many planktivorous predators. Cowfish are an example of a fish that continues to use spines as an adult. The same principle is used by puffers and porcupinefish, who are able to inflate rapidly when threatened. Although initially faced with a bite-sized meal, any predator approaching

Left: The cowfish's spiny projections make it more of a mouthful and deter predators.

these fishes is now confronted by something too large to swallow and is forced to withdraw.

Q: How else can spines be used?

A: Some fish use their spines more aggressively against attackers. Surgeonfish, for example, are named for the sharp, scalpel-like spines towards their tails that may be used in territorial disputes and against potential predators. Scorpionfish may also use their spines defensively. Triggerfish use the first two rays of their dorsal fin, not only in defence, but also to lock themselves into place in a reef crevice, thus preventing predators from ejecting them.

Q: Are any coral reef fish armoured?

A: Armour, in the form of toughened scutes on fishes' bodies, is a common defence in freshwater catfish. It is a much less common trait in reef fishes, possibly because such heavy armour seriously limits the ability of fish to move freely, making armoured fish far less effective at foraging in the highly competitive reef community. In addition to this, armour only deters a small number of predators; the largest reef hunters are very unlikely to be deterred by a tough skin – they simply eat the fish whole. Nonetheless, many larval reef fishes are heavily armoured – for their size – but lose this thick dermal protection as they settle on the reef. Amongst the plankton, this armour protects against some of the danger, but has little benefit once the young fish joins the adult community. Some reef fish do use armour throughout their lives; for example, the slow-swimming boxfish is almost impregnable to attack behind the tough skin and bony plates on its flanks.

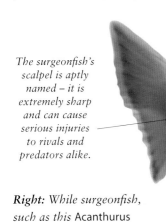

The surgeonfish's scalpel is aptly named – it is extremely sharp and can cause serious injuries to rivals and predators alike.

Right: *While surgeonfish, such as this* **Acanthurus japonicus,** *seem inoffensive and vulnerable, they are quite capable of inflicting wounds using extremely unusual weaponry!*

Sea shells

There are something like 150,000 known species of invertebrates in the world's seas and a large number can be found on coral reefs. Of these species, two groups dominate: the molluscs, which include marine snails, clams and even cephalopods, such as octopuses and cuttlefish; and the crustaceans, represented mainly by prawns, shrimps and crabs. Whereas soft-bodied inverts may use poisons or, like tubeworms, construct shelters, both molluscs and crustaceans typically use their hard outer shells to protect their vulnerable bodies.

Q: How thick is thick enough for a shell?

A: Any animal that protects itself from predators with a shell is faced with a conundrum: the more it invests in a heavy shell, the more difficult it becomes to move. Conches have come up with an excellent solution to this problem: the nobbles and hornlike projections that cover their shells make it all but impossible for their predators to get enough of a grip to crush them. Active crustaceans, such as

prawns, have comparatively thin shells, which are segmented to permit flexibility, while the better-protected crabs lose some of their flexibility as a result of their armour. Hermit crabs manage to retain their bodily flexibility by having comparatively thin shells. By sequestering snail shells to

protect them, the hermits can afford to be fairly soft bodied. Only their claws, which defend the opening to their shells, are heavily armoured.

Above: The crab's enormous claws provide sufficient muscle power to get through the shells of their prey.

Left: The irregular shape of this conch shell makes it all but impossible for a predator to get a good grip on it.

A shell inside

A tough outer shell offers protection, but severely limits movement – a real disadvantage for predators such as squid, octopus and cuttlefish.

The cuttlefish's shell within its body provides support for internal structures.

Q: How can predators get through a shell?

A: Even the toughest shell faces serious examination from the predators. Mantis shrimps can punch their way through it, while various whelk species can drill through a shell using powerful acids and mechanical drilling. Starfish can prise open the shell of a bivalve, such as a clam, by overcoming the muscles used to hold the shell closed. Populations of shelled invertebrates that live amongst many predators tend to have thicker shells for extra protection than those that exist in low-predation zones.

Q: If an octopus is a mollusc, why doesn't it have a shell?

A: Molluscs are an extremely diverse group that includes clams and mussels, as well as nudibranchs, octopuses and cuttlefish. There is clearly a wide range of different body designs within this group. The former have hard external shells, but what about the latter examples? Perhaps surprisingly, nudibranchs, octopuses and cuttlefish do have shells, but over evolutionary time they have been internalised; their shells are found within the animal's body. These light shells

Below: Starfish rely on the tough outer cuticle for protection as they patrol the reef, searching for food.

offer little protection, but do provide support for the body.

Q: What about other shell-less invertebrates?

A: Plenty of reef invertebrates lack a tough outer shell, so how do they protect themselves? Some, such as the echinoderms (starfish and sea urchins), have tough outer cuticles that allow a fairly free range of movement while providing an element of protection. Many others, such as coral polyps, construct their own shelters, either out of limestone that they produce themselves, or by gluing together small particles of sand and gravel. Many worms do this, so that they can withdraw to protect themselves when danger threatens. Softer-bodied invertebrates, such as nudibranchs, rely instead on chemicals for their protection.

Chapter 6
Shoaling

A large number of different fishes group together into shoals; it is estimated that over half of the 25,000 or so known fish species shoal at some stage during their lives. The widespread use of this strategy amongst fish is an indication of its value.

Shoaling behaviour provides each individual fish with a refuge from predators, helps it to find food more easily and, because of the hydrodynamic advantages of swimming in a group, can even save it energy.

Q: When is a shoal a school?

A: Not unsurprisingly, people are often confused by the two apparently competing terms – shoal and school – for a group of fish. The convention among fish biologists is to refer to a group of fish generally as a shoal. When fish are described as 'schooling' or being in a 'school', the individuals tend to be more closely knit as a unit, more polarised – all facing or swimming the same way – as opposed to shoaling, where the group is much less cohesive. Because shoaling is a broader term and infers less about what the fish are doing, we shall use

this term, rather than the more specialist 'school'.

Q: Which fish shoal and which do not?

A: Shoaling is a strategy used to different extents by different fish. A few species, such as herring, are known as 'obligate' shoalers – they are compelled to live in the social group and will rapidly die if isolated. Most social tropical marine species are 'facultative' shoalers, using the advantages of shoaling when it suits them and disbanding at other times, say, when there is a scramble for food. Many reef fishes use shoaling during the stages in their lives when they are particularly vulnerable to predators, such as when they have newly settled on the reef as juveniles. Often, they abandon the strategy as they grow larger and older, although some, such as green chromis, continue to shoal throughout their lives. Shoaling is most often

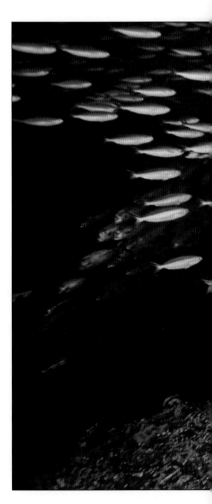

used by open-water species, especially planktivores, rather than those that live very close to the reef surface, such as blennies.

Below: *Huge shoals of fish gather to feed at the seaward edge of the coral reef. Jacks cruise in groups of between 10 and 100 fish, but shoals of fish such as fusiliers can number tens of thousands.*

Q: *When do fish choose to shoal or go it alone?*

A: Shoaling works extremely well as an anti-predator strategy but it also has costs. Living in a group means that fish must fight many competitors for their share of resources. So they tend to form shoals when they feel threatened, say, when a predator is around, when they move into new and unfamiliar environments or when they are in open water with no nearby hiding places to dash to. Furthermore, shoaling also only works against visual predators – those that hunt using sight. At night, fish shoals often tend to break up because concentrated shoals of fish attract hunters that use smell.

How shoaling works

Shoals of fish can comprise just two or three fish or over one million. Some species form huge aggregations; shoals of grey mullet in the Caspian Sea may extend for an incredible 100km. But irrespective of the species in question or the size of the shoal it forms, the basic principles about shoals are the same.

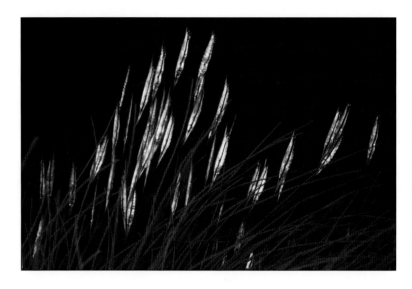

Q: *How do fish form shoals?*

A: Individual fish gather into shoals; they gravitate and are held together by 'social attraction'. Amongst fish such as shrimpfish (*Aeoliscus* sp.), this exerts an extremely powerful pull; individuals are strongly drawn to members of their own species and even to individuals of other, closely related species. If a shoal of fish is attacked and the members scatter, individuals sometimes become isolated. When this happens, solitary fish try to locate others by sight or by longer-range chemical cues. If and when they detect these cues, they rapidly home in on their source and rejoin the shoal. Similarly, shoals break up

Above: Shrimpfish adopt a head-down posture, packed together near the substrate and swaying in the current. This strange posture may serve to confuse predators.

as darkness falls each evening but reform at dawn every day as individual fish seek out and stick together with conspecifics. Large aggregations of nocturnal fish, such as cardinalfish and squirrelfish, gather under overhanging coral heads and in underwater caves during the day. These fish are attracted both by the shelter itself – individual fish remain faithful to the same resting place for long periods – as well as to the fish within.

Q: *How close do fish within a shoal get to one another?*

A: From the smallest fish to the huge pelagic species such as tuna, fish in shoals almost always maintain a steady distance between themselves and their nearest neighbours. This distance relates to the length of the fish; typically, fish in shoals tend to keep between two and three body lengths apart under normal circumstances. This means that in a shoal of 2cm-long fish, each one will leave a distance of between 4 and 6cm between itself and its nearest neighbours. These distances are governed

Attracting and repelling

Shoals are held together by social attraction, the force that makes individual members of shoaling species gravitate closer to one another.

by the situation that fish find themselves in; shoals tend to become more spread out when fish are hungry and scouring their habitat for food. By contrast, fish group together into tight shoals when threatened or when swimming against a fast current.

Q: *How do fish keep their shoals together?*

A: Fish use all their sensory abilities to keep tabs on their shoalmates. Smell is important for recognising shoal members and for locating the shoal if it moves out of sight. The sensation of touch, via the lateral line, is essential if fish are to polarise and move coherently with the rest of the shoal. However, the most important sensory input comes from the eyes; fish

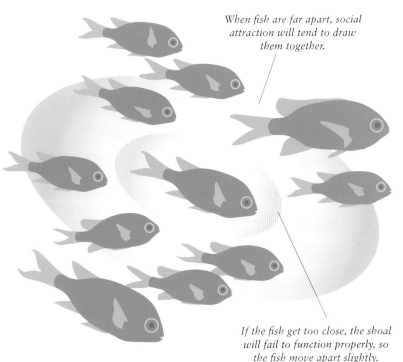

When fish are far apart, social attraction will tend to draw them together.

If the fish get too close, the shoal will fail to function properly, so the fish move apart slightly.

primarily use vision to maintain contact with the shoal, especially in the clear waters of the reef. It may also be that marine shoaling species signal to one another using fin flicks, as their freshwater fish do, in order to promote the cohesion of the shoal.

Left: Nocturnal soldierfish (Myripristis sp.) gather into huge aggregations in underwater caves, emerging at night to feed.

Synchronised swimming

One of the most arresting sights in the whole animal kingdom is that of a shoal of fish turning this way and that in perfect harmony with their shoalmates. It seems almost impossible to believe that animals could execute such a well-choreographed routine so beautifully, and yet they do. Of course, this impression is slightly exaggerated. What looks to be an extremely complicated and choreographed behaviour is in fact beautifully simple, and it is this simplicity that underlies its success. When it comes down to the nuts and bolts of shoaling behaviour, the fish are simply responding to localised cues. The effect this produces is no less beautiful but much easier to understand.

Q: So how do fish in shoals stay in such perfect synchrony?

A: No matter how large a shoal, each fish in it has relatively few near neighbours. The behaviour of these nearby fish exerts a strong influence on each individual fish, which simply copies its neighbours. For example, when a shoal meets an underwater obstacle or encounters a danger, the turning movement almost always begins with a single fish, or at most a small number of fish. Those nearest the turning fish will, in the absence of other information, replicate that movement. Then those next to them also turn and in this fashion the signal transmits across the whole shoal. Slowed right down using video footage, it is possible to see a wave of activity passing through the shoal, a phenomenon sometimes known as the 'Trafalgar effect'. During the Battle of Trafalgar,

> ▶ **Swimmingincircles**
>
> Shoals in the open waters off coral reefs sometimes form into tall columns that look like whirlwinds, as thousands of fish gather and swim in circles. This structure, called a 'torus', can last for hours, as the fish relax and swim around an empty core of water.

flags communicated messages from one ship to another throughout the fleet like a domino topple. The most amazing thing about a shoal

Shoals changing direction

A change in direction by one group member can spread throughout that group and be copied by group members in fractions of a second.

1 *An external influence, perhaps a predator or the smell of food, is detected by the leader.*

2 *The leader's response is to turn and take a new course, cutting across those swimming behind.*

Left: *A tightly packed shoal of* Chromis *align and travel together in the same direction. If a sufficient number of the leading fish were to turn and change direction, the rest of the shoal would swiftly follow.*

turning like this is the speed with which the signal to turn moves through the shoal. This rapid response is brought about in part by the need of each individual fish not to stand out from the crowd; those that do may often be picked out by a predator (see page 124).

Q: So does the shoal act more like a single, large animal than just a collection of individuals?

A: In some respects, yes. Although each fish has its own identity, the shoal sometimes seems to operate as if it had a

life of its own. This is particularly apparent in the way a shoal senses its environment. Shoals of fish are excellent at sensing the various stimuli in their environment; they are far better at it than if they were simply a loose collection of individual fish. If different members of the shoal detect the odour of food and each turns towards it, not all will be totally accurate in their course, but the average direction that all the detecting fish set a course for – the direction in which the shoal will eventually head – is usually extremely precise. This effect, sometimes referred to as the 'wisdom of crowds', is often seen in humans.

3 *This turning motion is usually then copied by the fish nearest to the leader.*

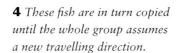

4 *These fish are in turn copied until the whole group assumes a new travelling direction.*

Safety in numbers

The single most important benefit that fish gain from shoaling is thought to be reducing their risk of predation. As a method of confounding hunters, shoaling works in a number of ways but the net effect – survival of the shoal members – has been shown again and again.

Q: What chance does a predator have of sneaking up on a shoal?

A: To hunt successfully, most predators need the element of surprise. They must approach sufficiently close to their quarry so that when they attack, their victim has no opportunity to flee. But as we have already seen, the sensory abilities of all the individuals in a shoal combine to provide excellent long-range detection. Because of its 'many eyes', a shoal of fish is likely to be aware of approaching danger, even before the predator has detected the shoal itself. For example, groups of zooplanktivores, including anthias, wrasse and damsels, which forage in the current during the day, dive for cover when they spot a predator approaching.

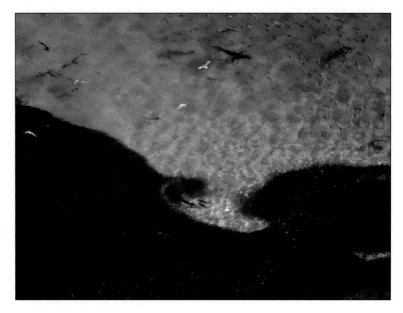

Q: What is meant by the 'confusion effect'?

A: Although some predators attack blindly, rushing at the shoal in the hope of snagging a fish at random, this approach is rarely effective. Instead, hunters usually try to select a victim before attacking, picking out an individual and chasing it down. Therefore, grouping fish select their shoalmates with care, strongly preferring to associate with conspecifics of the same size and colour, which produces shoals of near-identical fish. Faced with such a mass of

Above: The oceans play host to some enormous shoals of fish, such as these anchovy. Such huge shoals attract predators, yet the anchovies fare better than they would alone.

like-for-like fish, the predator is overloaded with choice and becomes 'confused'. This often has the effect of delaying an attack or causing the predator to abandon it altogether. However, if one shoal member has chosen its shoalmates poorly and is somehow different from the others, for example by being larger than them, the predator can often overcome the confusion effect and catch that fish. Shoaling fish that are in any way different are consequently at huge risk of being picked out, which is why they are all so similar in their colour patterns, body shape and even behaviour.

Q: *How else might shoaling help individual fish to survive predators?*

A: One important benefit of being in a shoal is known as 'attack dilution'. Most predators are only capable of capturing one victim at a time. Even if a predator makes a successful attack, a fish in a shoal of 100 others has only a 1% chance of being unlucky, so the risk of being the chosen one is diluted amongst the members of the shoal. The huge numbers of nocturnal fish that gather into daytime resting places divides the risk very effectively; the risk to any one of them during any single attack is relatively small. So in a risky situation it pays to be in the largest shoal possible. When reef fishes settle onto the reef, they face danger from all quarters. To reduce their risk, juvenile French grunts join shoals of mysid shrimps. At this stage, the grunts are almost transparent – much like the mysids. The fish even behave like mysids, making them less conspicuous to predators amongst the mass of shrimps. How do the fish repay the shrimps for using them as a shelter? They eat them – picking off the smallest members of the shrimp shoal!

Below: A predator has almost no chance of sneaking up unawares on a shoal of this size and a long-range attack is doomed to failure.

The costs and benefits of shoaling

Although shoaling is often thought of as a means of defeating predators, the combined senses of many individuals in the group also prove excellent at locating food patches in their environment. The result is that fish in shoals find food a great deal faster than if they hunted alone. And there are other benefits to shoaling: for example, fish in travelling shoals also save considerable amounts of energy by swimming in the slipstream of leading fish.

Q: *Are there any costs to shoaling behaviour?*

A: Set against all these advantages, there is one major cost – competition. Fish in shoals live amongst their greatest competitors. Although shoals are good at locating food, there is rarely enough to go around amongst all the shoal members

Below: Fish shoals change according to the conditions they experience: they pack tightly together if threatened, but spread out when there is food around.

and this means that all but the most dominant fish are left hungry. This can be a significant cost, so fish must weigh up the pros and cons of shoaling according to the situation.

Q: *How do fish decide when to shoal and when to go it alone?*

A: In each situation they experience, shoaling fish are fairly well able to assess the risks. If danger is lurking they very seldom actively choose to leave the safety of the shoal, but if a situation does not appear to be especially risky – and if they are hungry – fish may venture away from the group to try to find some food for themselves. Conversely, some fish are more successful at foraging when they are in a shoal; ocean surgeonfish (*Acanthurus bahianus*) that live in such groups are able to spend less time keeping an eye out for predators, meaning they can spend far more time foraging at their leisure. However, it can be advantageous to forage alone, especially for nocturnal fish. Shoaling works mainly to confound predators that hunt by sight. After dark, the smell of

large groups of fish can attract predators and the 'many eyes' defence is much less effective. This means that fish are rarely found in shoals at night – even those that spend the day in huge resting aggregations split up and go their own way after nightfall.

Q: *Do fish shoal right throughout their lives?*

A: Some do and some don't. Shoaling is most useful for fishes that do not live in very close proximity to the surface of the reef. Some species, such as Moorish idols, may shoal throughout their lives, while others, such as anthias, form into large shoals to feed and, later, to breed. Quite a few species shoal at some points in their lives and not at others. Parrotfish very often live in shoals as juveniles, only to switch to a more solitary, territorial life as they grow older and become sexually mature. Blue tangs follow a similar pattern, being gregarious during their earlier life and territorial loners later on. But why is this? It is simply because their priorities change. During the most vulnerable early stages of their existence, shoaling can provide an excellent refuge from danger. As the blue tangs grow, their need for this

protection decreases. As they mature, they need to establish their own territory in order to guarantee their food supply and, ultimately, to breed. However, when territories are hard to come by, as can happen when population densities are high and all territories are taken, either by conspecifics or by other grazers, adult blue tangs sometimes form

Above: Fish such as anthias (Pseudanthias *sp.) may gather for protection, but this does not signify harmony between shoal members – conflicts are common.*

into large groups to allow them to gain access to these defended resources. In these conditions, adults in shoals feed far more successfully than loners.

Life in the shoal

Shoals of fish are not fixed entities. They may change in size, going from thousands of individuals during the day to a complete disintegration at night, or splitting into two or more smaller groups. Nor are shoal members all equal – some benefit more by being in the shoal than others, often according to their position. There may be dominance hierarchies within the shoal and, while all may look peaceful to us, there may even be occasional outbreaks of aggression.

Q: *How does position in a shoal affect fish?*

A: Shoaling fish must balance the safety that the group provides against the cost of sharing their food. This does not necessarily mean that they must leave the shoal if they want to eat well or that their only chance of avoiding being eaten is to stick like glue to their shoalmates. Fish can move to different positions within the shoal because the benefits and the costs change according to whether they are at the front or the back, the middle or the edge. Fish at the

edge of a shoal get the first pick of the food and can take the tastiest morsels for themselves, while those at the centre of the group have to be content with the scraps. But to balance this, studies on groups of damselfish have shown that the fish at the edge are also at a greater risk of being captured by a predator. This means that hungry fish tend

to move to the dangerous, but food-rich margins of the shoal, returning to the centre when they are satiated. Amongst shoals of planktivorous fish, the larger individuals, who can swim faster to escape danger, usually occupy the best – and most dangerous – foraging positions constantly, even fighting off others who try to reach them. The huge

Position in a shoal

The position a fish occupies in its shoal dictates both its risks and its rewards, so fish tend to change their position according to their priorities.

Staying in the centre reduces the risk for fish – the more bodies between a fish and its predator, the safer it is.

Going to the front rewards a fish with the lion's share of the food, but puts it in danger, too.

feeding shoals formed by lyretail anthias are made up mostly of females and juveniles. Aggressive, dominant males defend patches of reef within the shoal and force rival, subordinate males to occupy dangerous and poorly supplied positions towards the bottom of the group.

Q: Do the fish co-operate or are they selfish?

A: When a shoal of fish is threatened, the fish on the outside try to reach the comparative safety of the middle. However, those already in the middle have no desire to be pushed to the outside, so they hold their ground. The net effect is that the shoal becomes highly compact. These attempts to hide behind other members of the group, to reach the safety of the centre of the group at the expense of others who are pushed into harm's way, was termed 'selfish herd' behaviour by the biologist Bill Hamilton.

Q: How does life in the shoal change over a day?

A: Shoals can change rapidly over short spans of time: some members may leave or new fish join so that the size of the group changes considerably; or the spacing of the fish in the shoal may change, the fish become more spread out as they search for food, but draw closer together if a predator threatens. The characteristics of a shoal can also change according to what

Above: Sergeant majors stream across the seagrass beds of a coral lagoon. Such mass movements are typical as shoals transfer between their feeding and resting grounds at different times of day.

the fish are doing. Grunts form into large, tightly packed shoals while they rest through the day (even within the shoal, some fish aggressively defend tiny patches of territory to ensure that they keep closest to a refuge). The shoal stays together into the evening, when it serves to protect group members as they migrate to their feeding grounds amongst the seagrass beds. However, once in the grass beds, the need for protection is much reduced and the shoal fragments as each fish goes its own way.

Who's who in the fish shoal

For fish that live in shoals, just as in human society, it pays to choose your associates carefully. In fact, it could be said to be even more important to fish than to people, because the wrong choice for a fish could put it at risk of being eaten!

Q: *What sort of things do they look at when deciding on a shoalmate?*

A: When a fish is deciding whether to join a shoal, it assesses the appearance of the existing shoal members. Given a choice, it prefers to shoal with fish of the same species as itself. After this it favours fish that are the same size and colour. Quite a few reef species exist in different colour morphs. Threadfin anthias, for example, occur in at least two different geographical colour types. The orange-and-red form shoals with similarly coloured flame anthias, whereas the purple-and-yellow colour morph shoals with Evan's anthias. Careful selection of shoalmates means fish groups are often composed of remarkably similar individuals, presenting predators with a confusing front of uniformity.

Q: *Are shoals of reef fishes often made up of more than one species?*

A: Yes; in general, the protection offered by a shoal is related to the size of the shoal, so by joining forces with similar-looking species, fish can benefit from participating in really large shoals. This happens in the Caribbean, for instance, where large groups of grunts, goatfish and snappers mass together above the reef. These mixed shoals can also be better at detecting predators or food than single-species shoals, because they have a spread of different sensory abilities. For example, one species may have a weak sense of smell but excellent vision, while another species has a better sense of smell but comparatively weaker vision. For these reasons, shoals across the reef are sometimes made up of a

Below: Shoaling fish are safest in larger shoals. If there are too few conspecifics about, fish will sometimes resort to shoaling with a different species entirely. This works most effectively when the two species look alike. The threadfin anthias (Nemanthias carberryi, left) has a variety of different guises, enabling it to mimic the appearance of the species that it shoals with, in this case Evan's anthias (Pseudanthias evansi, right).

hotchpotch of different fish, but if a predator hoves into view such shoals very often miraculously separate into sub-groups of matching fish, or if there are few conspecifics in the shoal, they may opt to dash for cover.

Q: Do fish always shoal with the same individuals?

A: It seems very likely. Fish in the wild often have very stereotypical movement patterns, especially as adults. They frequently use the same resting or feeding places and share the same migration routes. This means they have the potential to come into contact with the same individual fish on a regular basis as they go about their everyday lives. All the evidence points towards fish being able to recognise specific individual identities, but as yet it is unclear whether they prefer to shoal with these 'familiar'

Above: Although it seems that Banggai cardinalfish do not shoal with their relations, they do select closely matched individuals.

individuals over strangers. While this is still unknown, researchers have looked at whether relatives keep together in kin groups, but studies on both Banggai cardinalfish and the lyretail anthias have not found any evidence that fish prefer to stick with relatives.

Chapter 7
War and peace

To the casual observer, a tropical marine aquarium can seem the calmest of places, its inhabitants a living picture of serenity. But this is often an illusion; nature can be just as red in tooth and claw within the aquarium as it is beyond its glass walls.

Part of the skill of the aquarist is to select individuals and species that are compatible with one another. Even so, within the confines of the aquarium, reef animals will still very often squabble amongst themselves. Understanding what they might fight over and why is important if we are to create an environment in which they can prosper. But against this background of continual strife, there are quite a few examples of animals co-operating, providing assistance to one another in the day-to-day struggle for survival. There are compelling arguments to suggest that reef animals are master strategists, fighting when they have to and combining forces at other times. Here, we examine the strategies they use, from aggression to co-operation.

Below: Aggressive displays often include a gaping mouth. The fangs of this grouper (Plectropomus sp.) *could inflict serious wounds!*

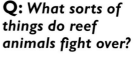

A large mouth is an intimidating sight.

Q: What sorts of things do reef animals fight over?

A: Animals almost always fight over the same thing – scarce resources. Be it food, space or mates, fights break out when there is not enough to go around. At stake is a claim for the lion's share of the available supplies. How hard animals fight depends on what is at stake – if it is only a meal, the battle will be far less fierce than when both struggle for the attentions of a mate or a precious territory.

Q: How do fish settle their disputes?

A: Actual fighting is comparatively rare. Although they may bicker and peck at one another fairly frequently, full-scale fights do not happen every day. When a dispute arises between fish, the protagonists usually engage in protracted displays towards one another. These displays convey to an opponent everything it needs to know about how tough its task will be if it continues to be aggressive. Most disputes are settled during this stage; it is only when two opponents are very closely matched that these preliminary displays fail to settle a score and that real fights break out.

Q: How about inverts – do they fight?

A: The same principles apply to invertebrate species. If there is a prize at stake and fighting can secure a greater share, then a struggle is likely to ensue. You might imagine that sessile invertebrates, such as corals, do not fight amongst themselves, but you would be mistaken.

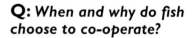

Above: Two valentine puffers (Canthigaster valentini) square up to one another in a ritualised show of aggression.

Q: When and why do fish choose to co-operate?

A: There are many instances when animals team up to accomplish things they would be unable to achieve on their own, from defending a territory and raising offspring to getting rid of parasites. Co-operation was once thought to be a relatively rare phenomenon, but as more cases come to light it has become apparent that it represents a vital part of the behavioural repertoire of many reef animals.

Left: Predators such as snake eels are often accompanied by other carnivores snatching at fleeing prey.

Food fights

If you were to reduce a fish's behaviour down to the basics, you would see that just about all of it stems from three main imperatives: the fish's need to avoid predators, to feed on a day-to-day basis and to breed successfully over the course of its life. Fish have plenty of ingenious strategies for avoiding predators and for breeding, but gathering energy to support the rest of their behaviour is no less challenging.

Above: Sit-and-wait predators, such as frogfish, protect ambush sites against intruders. Here, Antennarius pictus (left) defends its territory from A. nummifer.

Q: *With so many types of food available, why do fish get aggressive?*

A: Fish of different species feed on just about every kind of available organic matter, from a huge variety of animals and plants to the detritus that gathers at the bottom of the water column. But with the high densities of animals living on a coral reef, all fish face competition for their food from members of their own species, as well as others. Those who can gain the largest share of food for themselves are also the most likely to be successful at avoiding predators and, ultimately, breeding. With such a lot at stake

it is perhaps not surprising that the foragers are prepared to fight for their share.

Q: *When are feeding fish at their most aggressive?*

A: There are three main conditions under which fish are most likely to fight for food and all have to do with economics; if fish can get more food by fighting for it, then there is a

pretty good chance that they will. In places on coral reefs where both food resources and fish are concentrated, such as the so-called spur and groove zones on the seaward sides of some reefs, much more squabbling and harassment occurs between grazing fish, such as tangs and some damsels. Planktivorous fish, such as anthias, are less likely to fight on the open reef, because to do so would restrict their opportunities to feed in the current. However, what does happen in these fish is that larger, dominant individuals take up the best positions for feeding and keep their weaker counterparts at bay with some well-timed charges. In larger aggregations of these fish, a pattern often develops where the youngest fish are restricted to the rear of the group, but no single individual has enough time to devote to attacking all corners, so aggression is usually lower in large groups.

Q: Who is most likely to win a fight over food?

A: Size counts for a great deal in all types of fish fights – large fish are usually dominant. This is certainly the case in humbug damselfish, where the larger fish manage to pack away far more food than their smaller competitors. This is most likely because large fish can not only cover more ground when they are foraging, but can also muscle out small conspecifics from the best feeding grounds. The same rule applies in cleaning gobies; again, large fish will not tolerate the presence of weaker gobies at the richest foraging sites. As a result, subordinate fish must sometimes expose themselves to more risk to get their food or change their diets. There is a considerable amount of anecdotal evidence to suggest that in species ranging from angelfish to tangs, the strongest competitors can monopolise the best food patches, be they algal mats or sites rich with the juiciest invertebrates. This leaves the weaker fish to feed at other places where they must settle for less nutritious prey. Another downside for the weaker fish is that in their desperation to find food they may have to forage in risky areas. For example, juvenile anthias are forced to forage in parts of the reef where predators are most likely to concentrate their attacks.

Left: For male Pseudanthias hypselosoma, *gaining and holding a territory means a guaranteed supply of food, plus access to females and to hiding places.*

Territories on the reef

The coral reef is home to huge numbers of animals, each seeking to gather food, to shelter and to find suitable space to breed. But these resources are scarce; there is rarely sufficient to go around so the competition is intense. Under these conditions, the only way that reef fish can guarantee their supplies is to exclude their rivals and defend a territory that allows them private access to the resources they need. The exact requirements vary from species to species; some fish defend only their foraging patches, others include a sheltered nest site within their territory.

Q: *How large are fish territories?*

A: Fish territories vary considerably in size. Fish such as grunts, that rest throughout the day before dispersing to feed with the onset of night, defend territories containing hiding places that may be as small as a 20cm square. Moray eels are equally aggressive in defence of refuge holes. At the other end of the spectrum, some triggerfishes

How much is enough?

Fish territories vary hugely in size. Some species defend small, localised areas, whereas others assert their rights over huge stretches of reef.

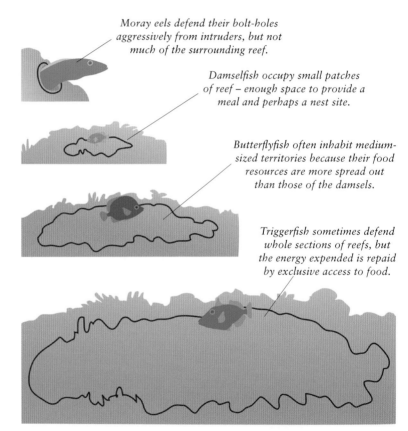

Moray eels defend their bolt-holes aggressively from intruders, but not much of the surrounding reef.

Damselfish occupy small patches of reef – enough space to provide a meal and perhaps a nest site.

Butterflyfish often inhabit medium-sized territories because their food resources are more spread out than those of the damsels.

Triggerfish sometimes defend whole sections of reefs, but the energy expended is repaid by exclusive access to food.

defend enormous territories of up to 200m². Territory size also varies between members of the same species – the larger the territory, the more food it will provide for its owner.

However, this comes at the cost of increased work in defending it, so only the strongest individuals can defend the largest and best territories. The cost of defending a territory increases when there are more competitors to fight off. The territories of dusky gregorys (*Stegastes nigricans*) tend to be larger in winter, when there are fewer competitors, than in high-density summer conditions.

Q: Where's the best place to have a territory?

A: For a fish to go to the extent of defending a territory – a behaviour that uses up considerable time and energy – there has to be considerable benefit. The territory must provide the fish with plenty of food and that food usually has to be renewable. For herbivorous fish, such as damsels, the best site for a territory is one where the algae can gain the most light possible, which usually means shallow surface waters. Under these conditions, the alga grows slowly but continuously, providing a steady harvest for the fish that is prepared to defend it. Research has shown that many damselfishes actively culture an algal garden, weeding out some of the faster-growing but less nourishing species of algae in favour of other types, which are richer in nutrients. Their effectiveness in achieving this is shown when fish are experimentally excluded from patches of reef – the fishes' carefully cultivated salad gardens are rapidly overgrown by the algal equivalent of weeds.

Q: What else should a territory have?

A: It is essential that territories provide some cover – a bolt-hole for the fish to shelter in if a hunter comes along. For some fish, including clownfish, the protection provided by a territory – in their case an anemone – is the number one requirement. Sheltered areas are often also used for the safe deposit of eggs, as far as possible out of sight of sneaking egg predators. Damselfish defend territories that include grazing areas, shelters and, for some of the males, a nest site. In many cases this nest site is a small patch of red algae that may be cultured by the male. Once he finds a satisfactory site, the male can remain in place for several years. The importance to a male of having the 'full package' in terms of a territory was suggested by a study on the blue-striped fairy wrasse (*Cirrhilabrus temminckii*) where the female chooses her mate on the basis of the quality of his territory.

A little give and take

The size of a fish's territory is related to the competition in the area. The more competitors, the harder it is to keep every intruder at bay.

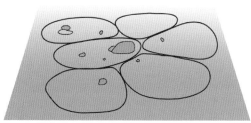

Winter *At this point in the year, fish densities are typically low and territories can expand to increase the available foraging area.*

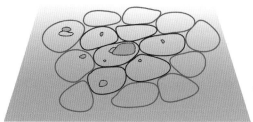

Summer *With more demand on space and more mouths to feed, territories shrink, but in good conditions a small area can supply as much food as a winter range.*

Territorial fish

Perhaps the majority of reef fishes, including many damselfish, butterflyfish, surgeons, tangs, parrotfish, triggers and groupers, stake out and defend territories to feed or to lay their eggs. For any strategy to be so routinely adopted it must provide considerable benefits, yet territoriality is often referred to as a 'density-dependent' strategy, meaning it only occurs when large numbers of fish are concentrated in a small area. When densities are low, fish usually do not bother to spend energy on defending a territory, but this is rarely the case on coral reefs.

Q: *How do fish gain possession of a territory?*

A: Finding and occupying a territory is an activity usually associated with the onset of adulthood. With age comes size, and with size comes power and increased competitive ability. This means that juvenile fish of most species must bide their time; for example, young parrotfish tend to live in groups. As they mature they go it alone, becoming solitary and starting to seek out

territories. In many species, such as the dusky gregory, younger fish are forced to gather in areas away from territorial adults and where food is comparatively scarce. For coral-dwelling gobies, such as the broad-barred goby (*Gobiodon histrio*) the size of the fish is directly related to the size of the territory; smaller individuals have to make do with equally small corals, while larger fish occupy the largest coral territories. When given

a free choice, fish of all sizes prefer to set up their territories in large corals, so the fact that smaller fish do not is due to competition. As fish grow they can trade up, fighting for better territories. However, one factor does count against them: to win a territory they must drive off the current owner who is, of course, on home ground. Studies have shown that where two competitors are equal, home advantage counts for a great deal.

Fish status symbols

The largest, most aggressive fish snap up the most desirable territories, while lower-ranking individuals have to make do with lesser residences.

Males with good territories are sought out by females.

Being small, limits the quality of territory a fish can hold.

Q: Are territorial fish equally aggressive to all other fish?

A: Fish with feeding territories save most of their aggression for fish with the same diet as themselves. Butterflyfish tolerate the presence of fish with different diets in their territories, but are quick to drive out direct competitors. It has been shown that a damselfish presented with an unknown fish is extremely quick to learn what the stranger eats and to tailor its aggression accordingly. Damselfish also show more aggression towards larger invaders, such as parrotfish and surgeonfish, that could have the greatest impact on their carefully tended algal gardens. Species such as Ward's damsel (*Pomacentrus wardi*) will happily tolerate the presence of fish such as the jewelled blenny (*Salarias fasciatus*) within their territories, possibly because this aggressive fish contributes to the damsel's territory defence by helping to keep out other blennies.

Q: What happens to fish that can't get territories?

A: When all available territories are taken, certain individuals, especially juveniles, are sometimes forced to follow

Above: The small jewel damsel is hostile towards direct competitors. To avoid aggression, young surgeonfish may mimic species that do not compete with the damsel.

other options. Failing to acquire a territory is bad news for fish and means that their food supply is likely to be heavily restricted. An experiment on fairy basslets showed that smaller fish were able to almost double their feeding rates when larger, more dominant individuals were absent from their reef. This is one reason why many fish, such as blue tangs, are differently coloured as juveniles; territorial adult reef fish tend to attack fish of the same colour as themselves. However, there are options available to

fish that fail to secure a territory. Where there are high densities of fiercely territorial damselfish, blue tangs often abandon attempts to defend their own territories and gang together to raid the damselfishes' territories en masse. The aggressive territorial defence of the jewel damsel (*Plectroglyphidon lacrymatus*) is thought to have driven juvenile chocolate surgeonfish (*Acanthurus pyroferus*) to mimic different species of pygmy angelfish. By doing this, the juvenile mimics are thought to deceive the damsels into thinking that they are, like pygmy angels, not direct competitors. Certainly the mimics suffer less aggression from the damsels and are able to spend more time feeding.

To defend or not to defend?

Defending a territory is an expensive business. A territorial fish has access to all the food its patch can supply, but must spend a large amount of time and effort in driving away possible intruders. When the benefits outweigh the costs, as can happen at certain times of the year, or even certain times of the day, fish may abandon their territories and adopt different strategies. Even when a territory is essential, say to maintain a breeding ground, fish have developed ways of cutting the costs of territory defence.

Q: *Do fish defend their territories constantly?*

A: Territory defence uses up a great deal of a fish's energy, so it only happens when the payback to the fish is high. If the amount of food that a territory produces starts to decline, then the benefit to the fish in defending that territory will also decline and the fish is likely to give it up and move on after a while. Some damselfish live in loose shoals during the early hours of the day, only to stake claims for territories and become aggressive in late morning and throughout the afternoon, before abandoning them and reverting to non-aggressive shoaling later in the day. It is thought that the reason for this lies with the nutritional value of the algae on which they feed. When the sun is at its peak, the algae respond by photosynthesising and producing large amount of sugars, making them especially delectable to the damselfish during these hours and rewarding their efforts in defending a territory.

Q: *How are territories spread across the reef?*

A: The largest and strongest fish are best suited to the hard

Neighbours at war

Dawn *At this time, there is little sign of direct aggression between the damsels as they gather into shoals above the reef to feed.*

Mid-day *Now, algal production is at its peak. Dominant damselfish establish territories and keep the rich food resources to themselves.*

Late afternoon *The nutritional value of the algae drops and the benefits of an exclusive territory decline. Gradually, shoals reform.*

Top of the heap

Where food and shelter are in abundance, territories are held by dominant fish. The other fish have to settle for less and await a vacancy.

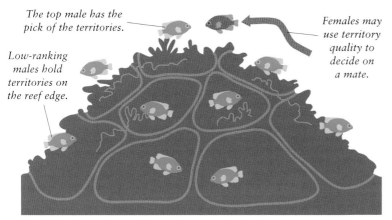

The top male has the pick of the territories.

Low-ranking males hold territories on the reef edge.

Females may use territory quality to decide on a mate.

work of winning and defending a good territory. Territories on the reef often build up into a mosaic across the surface. The best territories are usually found in the centre of the group, where food supplies such as algae are greatest and where fish can find cover. Other good territories may be arrayed around this, with poorer-quality territories on the outside of the reef, where they may be subject to attack by predators and have lower food supplies. A study on three-spot damselfish showed that males with central territories grew faster than their counterparts with edge territories. The central territories were richer in algae and also less at risk of a raid

party of intruders eating the precious food. More importantly, the central males attracted more females to lay eggs in their territories; female fish are good judges of territory quality and reward the efforts of a male who has staked his claim in a good territory by mating with him.

Q: How do fish deal with their boundary disputes?

A: The crowded nature of reef life means that territorial fish always have neighbours. While the territory is being established and boundaries are being worked out, neighbours can frequently become confrontational. This usually involves a great deal of

displaying and mock charging without the fish actually coming to blows, as each fish tries to impress upon the other that it is not to be messed with. But once the boundaries are determined and the relationship between neighbours is worked out, things tend to settle down. Boundaries are extremely important to fish and usually demarcated by landmarks, such as a piece of rubble or branched coral. When a territorial red-back butterflyfish (*Chaetodon paucifasciatus*) selects a new partner, the incoming fish rapidly learns where the boundaries are and, in doing so, prevents upheaval and an escalation in aggression. Damselfish quickly learn to recognise their neighbours and declare a truce. A fragile non-aggression pact seems to ensue, sometimes called the 'dear enemy' effect, that enables fish to avoid petty squabbling with the same few neighbouring individuals, while allowing them to defend vigorously against outsiders. The damsels are even able to tell the difference between the warning or aggressive sounds made by neighbours and those made by unfamiliar fish, responding more strongly to the newcomers in line with the greater threat that these may present to the territory.

Pecking orders

Although dominance hierarchies were first studied in domestic chickens – hence the term 'pecking order' – many different kinds of animals, fish included, fight amongst themselves to see who is boss. In the wild, these dominance hierarchies are usually formed between conspecifics, but in aquariums a hierarchy can often develop between the inhabitants, regardless of their species.

Q: Why do fish establish dominance hierarchies?

A: Hierarchies develop when individual fish attempt to stake a claim for a share of the resources, which in most cases means food. The largest and most aggressive fish are capable of out-competing others so they take a disproportionate chunk for themselves, leaving the others to squabble for what is left. Royal grammas (*Gramma loreto*) live in groups on the undersides of reef ledges and feed on drifting plankton. The best spots for gathering plankton are always held by dominant individuals in the group, who aggressively defend their place against subordinate fish. Although fighting for an elevated place in the hierarchy can be costly in the short run, the dominant fish gain their rewards over time, growing faster than lower-ranked fish and maturing sooner into breeding adults. However, subordinate fish also benefit from being in the group. Damselfish at the bottom of the pecking order grow comparatively slowly, but are less likely to be captured by predators because of the safety of being in a group.

Q: How do fish decide on their place in the hierarchy?

A: Fish decide an order of precedence through aggression and direct competition from the dominant individuals at the top of the hierarchy down to the weaker subordinate fish at the bottom. Dominance is usually determined by size, age and experience: larger fish boss small ones, older fish dominate younger ones, and fish that have been living in a particular locale for a period outrank newcomers. But for otherwise equal fish, the hierarchy may be decided by a great deal of displaying and even out-and-out fighting, although this is by no means the only method they use. Simply by watching others fight, fish can decide whether they have any real chance against the combatants. If they decide that one or other of the fighters is a real bruiser, they

Below: Fighting for a place in the pecking order is a serious business for fish such as royal grammas (Gramma loreto). Dominant fish get the lion's share both of food and breeding opportunities.

can save themselves from injury by signalling submissiveness to these fish in future. Perhaps the best predictor of a fish's position in a dominance hierarchy is its size, but even amongst closely matched fish the order is usually established extremely quickly, often within 24 hours.

Q: *What about hierarchies based on their members' sexes?*

A: A number of coral reef fish live in breeding groups where the sexes assume different positions in the dominance hierarchy. For example, some cleaner wrasse form so-called linear hierarchies, where each individual occupies a step on the ladder, dominant to those below it but subordinate to any above. (The alternative is the 'despotic hierarchy', sometimes seen in eels, where a single dominant individual aggressively rules the roost over all others, who are each of approximately equal rank.) In cleaner wrasse, the hierarchy is topped by a single dominant male and the other fish in the pecking order are all females, whereas in anemonefish (clownfish), the reverse is true; the female is at the top of the pile and the males form the remainder of the hierarchy.

How the hierarchy works

Although many coral reef fish form dominance hierarchies, the way this social system works varies considerably from species to species.

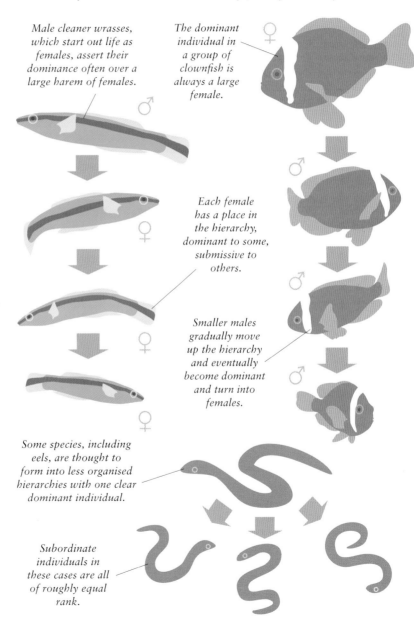

Male cleaner wrasses, which start out life as females, assert their dominance often over a large harem of females.

The dominant individual in a group of clownfish is always a large female.

Each female has a place in the hierarchy, dominant to some, submissive to others.

Smaller males gradually move up the hierarchy and eventually become dominant and turn into females.

Some species, including eels, are thought to form into less organised hierarchies with one clear dominant individual.

Subordinate individuals in these cases are all of roughly equal rank.

Fish fights: the lead-up

The aggressive nature of many tropical marine fish, particularly their intolerance for their own or similar species, can present a real problem for fishkeepers. Like all animals, fish must compete to acquire resources such as food, territories or mates. On the coral reef, food, hiding places, territories and mates are almost always in short supply. To acquire these precious commodities, or even just to hold on to what they have, fish must usually compete and this competition can often escalate into direct aggression. But actual fighting is extremely costly – even the victor can sustain serious injuries – so fish go to great lengths to size up their opposition, to try to scare their rival, to impress it into backing down, while all the time trying to work out their own chances of winning if it should come to a fight.

Q: How do fish decide whether or not to fight an opponent?

A: The likelihood of one fish attacking another individual is affected by two main factors. First of all, the fish will assess several physical characteristics of its rival in order to decide its chances of coming out on top. This usually means its opponent's size – fish are much more likely to attack small fry than a big bully. However, if a fish is defending precious eggs it is likely to throw caution to the wind and fearlessly attack members of species that are several times larger than itself. Some fish, such as triggerfish, will even attack divers! Secondly, the potential aggressor will determine the extent to which its rival presents a threat to its precious possessions: its food, territory or mates.

Q: What other characteristics do fish assess in their rivals?

A: Coral reef fishes tend to be most aggressive towards individuals that use the same resources – food and territories – as themselves, and the biggest competitive overlap is with members of their own species. Colour is extremely important, especially on the coral reef and fish tend to attack when confronted by an individual that is the same colour as themselves. Matching colours can indicate fish of the same or similar species that would compete for exactly the same resources. This matched colour aggression, seen in butterflyfishes, amongst others, is one reason why juvenile reef fish tend to be so differently coloured to adults of the same species – to discourage aggression. Similarly, some fish, including damsels, are known to attack fish according to their shape. This is because a

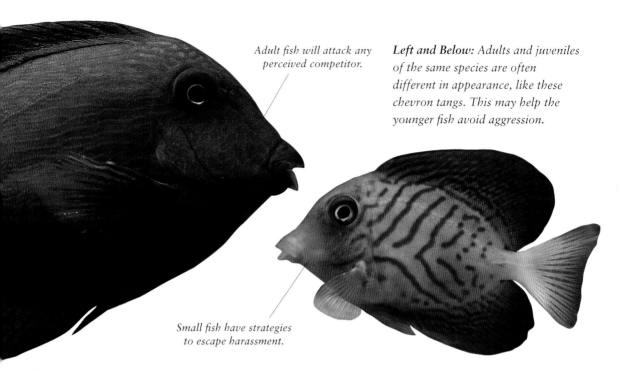

Adult fish will attack any perceived competitor.

Left and Below: *Adults and juveniles of the same species are often different in appearance, like these chevron tangs. This may help the younger fish avoid aggression.*

Small fish have strategies to escape harassment.

fish's shape, like its colour, gives a clue to its diet and therefore the threat it presents as a competitor. However, fish do not just rely on hard-and-fast rules for this. It has been shown that damselfish are able to learn what is, and what is not, a competitor, getting clues by watching the behaviour of other fish to work out what they are eating. As well as all this, male fish are sometimes more aggressive to other males than to females that stray into their territories. Some male wrasse and pygmy angels will ferociously exclude other males, while welcoming potential mates.

Picking your fights

Deciding who is a threat to your interests and who is not is important. Body shape and colour are clues to whether a fish is a competitor or not.

A differently coloured fish may pass the first test, but if it acts like a competitor it may be attacked.

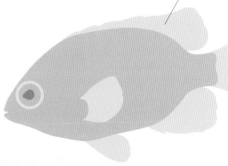

Fights: weighing up the opposition

When rival fish size each other up from afar, the most common outcome is that one of them will recognise the other's superiority and keep its distance, or be chased off without putting up any resistance. But when fish are fairly closely matched in terms of their size and motivation, then the aggression stakes are raised. This does not necessarily mean that a fight is inevitable – far from it. Out-and-out fights are rare because of the very real danger of serious injury, even for the victor. In most cases, disputes are settled by a series of ritualised displays and signals that are calculated to communicate the prowess of each fish without actual physical contact.

Q: *What form do these displays and signals take?*

A: The potentially deadly cost of injuries from fighting means that fish have evolved a wide range of different displays. The most obvious ones to a human observer are the visual displays that fish use at close quarters. For example, when rivals come

Above: In this stand-off between two male yellow shrimp gobies, fins are spread, bodies held rigid and mouths and gills held open.

their mouths wide. Damsels more usually display by spreading their dorsal and anal fins and swimming in a stiff, exaggerated manner. In doing so, they display their flanks to one another and often circle like tentative boxers. These visual displays are frequently backed up physically or by audible signals. Lateral displays are very often supported by each fish sharply contracting its muscles, causing its body to wave and sending a pulse of water towards the opponent. This allows each fish to assess its rival's strength very directly, via the pressure-sensitive lateral line. Most territorial reef fish, including butterflyfish and damsels, are also highly capable of making warning noises to rivals in exactly the same way as animals such as deer or lions.

Q: *What do the signals mean?*

A: The whole purpose of all the signals is to try to impress a rival. Spread fins act, if not to exaggerate, then at least to emphasise a fish's size. This is important because, nine times out of ten, a large fish will overcome a smaller opponent. Wide open mouths and flared gill covers attempt to achieve the same thing by demonstrating

size and power. Displaying by spreading the fins also maximises the impact of a fish's colour pattern, which is in turn related to its health and, again, its strength. The growls and grunts that different fish make also pass on information. Fish are highly attuned to small differences in these calls and can tell a great deal from them. Although it is possible for fish to make the most of themselves using displays, they cannot fake them outright. A fish cannot pretend to be twice the size it is nor develop strong colours without being in the peak of health, so all these displays are honest signals of a fish's quality.

Q: *How else might fish assess their opponents?*

A: Remarkably enough, fish can also pick up information about potential rivals by watching them in contests with others. These so-called bystander effects have been shown in male gobies, which adjust their level of aggression towards other males if they have been able to pick up information by watching them fight. When they are confronted with a fish that has just won an aggressive encounter – that has proved itself in a direct fight – they are less aggressive than when they face up to a loser!

face-to-face, they may flare their gill covers or, in the case of royal grammas and some gobies, open

Fights: getting down to business

If two closely matched fish fail to decide the issue by displays, an actual fight may develop, but this is relatively rare. Two aggressors must be very closely matched, with a great deal at stake, before they fight.

Q: How do fish make the transition from displaying to fighting?

A: Sometimes the transition from displaying to fighting can be rapid and dramatic, with a sudden flurry of aggression. At other times it is much more gradual, again reflecting the reluctance of fish to risk injury needlessly. Goatfish, for example, spar rather reservedly with their barbels. The protagonists come together face-to-face, almost like fencing partners, jabbing at each other with their extended barbels. For other species, the first stage in an actual physical contest is jaw-locking. This behaviour has been documented between female clownfish and different *Chromis* species. Jaw-locking usually involves a kind of tug-of-war, with each opponent trying to demonstrate its strength and superiority in a kind of physical extension of a display. Royal grammas perform this mouth-wrestling tenaciously, shaking their heads while locked in their embrace and sometimes tearing or otherwise damaging each other's mouthparts.

Q: What happens when a real fight starts?

A: This varies from fish to fish, but there are several common threads in all fishy altercations. For one thing, the combatants usually tend to target the same parts of their opponents' bodies. Top targets are often the fins, which makes sense because a torn fin is likely to slow down a foe. Any vulnerable part is also fair game; fish often attack the

Below: Trials of strength, such as the jaw-locking behaviour seen here between two twinspot Maori wrasse (Oxycheilinus bimaculatus), *allow fish to settle disputes without direct fighting.*

Battling butterflies

Copperband butterflyfish fight by ramming their heads together in a trial of strength, shoving hard to try and push each other backwards.

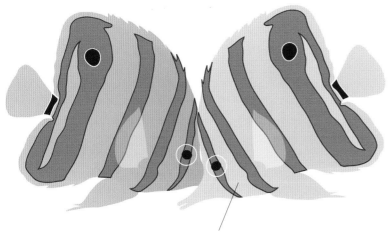

The losing fish can show its submission by changing the colour of its eyespot.

eyes and unprotected flanks of their enemies. Surgeonfishes and tangs have been known to bring their sharp tail spines to bear, wounding their opponent's flank. A full-blown fight rarely lasts more than a few seconds – or minutes at most. Once one fish has landed a few blows – or bites – the impulse to fight can rapidly leave the other and it may seek to break contact and flee.

Q: What happens after a fight?

A: Once the victor has been decided the losing fish must make itself scarce, otherwise its life might be at risk. The winner will not tolerate its presence in the immediate area and will continue to attack – no quarter is given. In the open waters of the reef, this is not often a problem, but in the confines of an aquarium, the constant harrying of the victor may prove fatal. Ultimately, this could be the fate of either of the fighters in the immediate aftermath of the battle, as open wounds may become infected – fighting is a costly business. If both survive and there is sufficient space to shelter the loser, the protagonists

are unlikely to fight again. Fish tend to remember the identity of their conquerors and do not make the same mistake twice.

Q: What makes certain kinds of fish so prone to aggression in the home aquarium?

A: Some species of fish, such as some angelfish, are notoriously testy in the home aquarium, but a great many fish will not tolerate the presence of conspecifics. One reason for this is the comparative shortage of space and hiding places in an aquarium. Many reef fishes in the wild defend enormous territories from members of their own species. For example, tangs may defend territories running into tens of square metres against conspecifics and food competitors alike. Fish are also more aggressive when defending their patch and prior residence counts for a great deal in fish contests. A newly introduced fish must cope not only with the change in habitat, but also the aggressive intentions of established tankmates. The job of the aquarist is to plan ahead in order to stock compatible fish and to ensure the availability of sufficient resources in terms of food and hiding places.

Fighting dirty – invertebrates

If you want to observe real aggression on a coral reef, you must look beyond the comparatively tame quarrels and spats between fishes and see what is happening on the surface of the reef amongst organisms such as anemones, sponges and the corals themselves. Here, competition for space is arguably even more intense; whereas fish can disperse in search of a territorial foothold, these invertebrate combatants are forced to fight or die.

Q: What strategies do corals use to gain the space that they require?

A: There are two main tactics available to corals in their continual battles with neighbouring colonies and species: they can either shade out their competitors by growing above them and cutting off the light that their symbiotic zooxanthellae need to photosynthesise; or they can use more attacking means to grab precious space. Fast-growing, branching corals can rise above the substrate and overshadow their competitors, cutting off

their light and restricting the supply of food particles, which mostly results in their death. But the slower-growing corals have some aggressive tricks to defend their space and move into pastures new.

Q: How can sponges and corals be aggressive?

A: It may be hard to imagine that either of these groups of animals can be aggressive in the way we understand it, but to survive on the reef, they must

Below: Hammer, or anchor, corals (Euphyllia *spp.*) *are notoriously aggressive towards other corals. As* Euphyllia *extends its range, it uses sweeper tentacles to damage or kill corals that lie in its way.*

fight their corner like any other organism. Corals may reach out towards neighbouring colonies with stinging sweeper tentacles and digestive filaments. The so-called hammer, or anchor, corals (*Euphyllia* spp.) are well known in the aquarium hobby for their aggressive use of stinger-packed sweeper tentacles that may extend outwards almost 25cm from the coral itself. These act quickly to inflict fatal damage or, in the case of digestive filaments, to dissolve the living tissue of polyps they contact, leaving space for the aggressor to invade. Sponges, which also encrust the reef, sometimes attack corals by excavating immediately beneath the coral polyps and thereby undermining – and killing – the living tissue.

aggression. Brain and pillar corals are quick to launch attacks on any neighbour that threatens to encroach on their space or light. Although these attacks are usually fatal, the fast-growing species can rapidly colonise new areas on the reef. This process of fast growth balancing out aggression helps to maintain the diversity of corals on a typical reef. However, this balance can be affected by local conditions, such as water flow, to produce large areas that are entirely dominated by a few species — or even just one.

Left: Here, a fast-growing soft coral (Rhytisma sp.) is rapidly smothering the more sedate branched Montipora sp. coral.

Q: Is there a dominance hierarchy amongst corals?

A: There are major differences in the rates at which different corals grow. Many branching corals are far faster growers than the more massive corals, such as brain coral. So how do the slower-growing colonies compete? Simply put, what they lack in speed they make up for in

Right: Access to light is essential for corals and their algae, so some species grow up and away from the reef, shading out their rivals.

Co-operation – space sharing

As we have seen, reef organisms often have to fight for a territory or food, but life on the coral reef is not all about aggression. Faced with this kind of extreme competition, many animals team up, co-operating with each other to boost their chances. There are different degrees of so-called co-operation between two animals, ranging from 'commensalism', where one partner gains a benefit from an interaction while the other neither gains nor loses, to 'mutualism' where both partners reap rewards from one another – the classic win-win situation. The most basic kind of commensalism occurs when one animal lives alongside – or even on – another.

Above: A pair of Coleman shrimp seek shelter in the spines of a sea urchin. Many reef animals use the defences of other species for their own benefit in this way.

Q: What kinds of reef organisms associate like this?

A: Large or poisonous animals provide excellent cover for small, bite-sized lodgers all over the reef. Nudibranchs – sea slugs – often carry within their tissues a lethal arsenal of toxins, rendering them safe from most predators. Moreover, they advertise their toxicity with bright warning colours. To small and vulnerable animals such as shrimps, or to tiny fish such as newly settled gobies, the nudibranchs represent an ideal refuge. For example, the imperial shrimp lives in the gills of a large sea slug known as a Spanish dancer, gaining both protection and food; the shrimp eats the slug's waste matter. Other species of shrimp live alongside sea cucumbers and corals, amongst other things, gaining protection and sometimes food, but usually without paying any kind of rent to their landlords.

Q: Do reef animals ever share their territories?

A: Territorial fish defend their patches aggressively from direct competitors, but are more sanguine about unrelated fish that pose them no threat. For example, large tangs and surgeonfish drive off other herbivores relentlessly, while allowing carnivorous species, such as wrasse and gobies, free passage. But the benefit to the smaller fish goes beyond just avoiding aggression; they frequently stay closely alongside the surgeonfish as it browses on its algal garden, feeding on the small invertebrates that it disturbs. A similar thing happens when goatfish feed on the substrate; the clouds of debris produced by the foraging goatfish attract other species, such as damsels, like magnets.

Below: Goatfish dig through the substrate in search of tasty morsels, attracting other fish to feed on the small animals they expose.

Q: *Do groups of the same species ever combine to defend joint territories?*

A: Territorial defence can sap energy and be highly time-consuming, and a shortage of available territories often means that there are not enough to go around. A solution to both these problems is to share a territory, spreading the workload and the benefits. Species that share in this way include cleaner wrasse and clownfish. In these examples, the territory often consists of a breeding pair and subordinate

helpers, or a male and his harem. In the case of striped parrotfish the room-mates are usually all unrelated females. A strict dominance hierarchy operates in these parrotfish territories; dominant individuals could drive out lower-ranked fish if they chose. The reason they do not is that the subordinate fish contribute to the territory's defence, allowing the dominant fish to spend more time feeding. It is not all sweetness and light, though – the dominant fish jealously hog the best food patches within the defended area.

Co-operation – mutualism

Co-operation can sometimes go beyond simple commensalisms and take the form of a real partnership – a mutualism. One dramatic example is the way that some species of fish and shrimps clean parasites from the skin of larger fish. The high densities of fish found on coral reefs gives rise to large numbers of lice and worms that live on the fish and draw their nutrition from them. At best, these infestations cause an irritation to the fish, at worst the parasites can seriously weaken their hosts. The cleaners therefore provide a vital service to other fish – usually referred to as their 'clients'.

Q: Which animals provide parasite cleaning?

A: Many different animals act as cleaners during a part of their lives. Various fish species, including the French angelfish

(Pomacanthus paru) and several wrasses and gobies, perform this role as juveniles and some shrimps also fulfil this function. But the most famous are fish such as the wrasse *Labroides dimidiatus*, which spends its entire life as a cleaner. It is extremely active and can clean over 2,000 fish in a single day.

Q: How does this work in practice?

A: Individual cleaner wrasse establish specific cleaning stations where they remain throughout the day, waiting for clients and aggressively defending these stations from other cleaner wrasse. And it is not just the

Above: A cleaner wrasse (Labroides dimidiatus) fusses over its client, here an emperor angelfish, looking for parasites.

Right: Many species of small fish, or even juveniles of larger species, show cleaner behaviour. Here, a Spanish hogfish (Bodianus rufus) cleans a creole wrasse.

cleaners that defend their stations; the clients themselves can sometimes end up queuing for the attentions of the wrasse. Where this happens, aggression can sometimes break out as fish try to jockey for priority. Amazingly, the cleaners can distinguish between clients whose own territoriality means they have to remain in one place and cannot visit another cleaning station, and clients who are free to move to other stations. These latter VIP clients are given priority treatment by the cleaners.

Below: This yellow tang is enjoying the attention of a cleaner shrimp (Lysmata amboinensis).

Q: *Is this true mutualism?*

A: While cleaners provide an undoubted benefit for their clients, they also occasionally supplement their diet by biting small chunks off them! Annoyed clients sometimes give chase, but remarkably, the cleaners provide them with a better service next time, showing that they are capable of individually recognising their clients. To try to prevent an aggressive client from pursuing the matter, the cleaners dash to the next client in line – often a predatory fish – and get to work on them. Cleaners also refrain from biting while a VIP client is waiting for service.

This is because fish in the queue watch the behaviour of previous clients and if those dash off suddenly, so do the queuing fish. However, cleaners are not so careful when only their territorial clients are queuing!

Q: *How do cleaner wrasse advertise to their clients?*

A: There is always a danger that a small fish, such as a cleaner wrasse, could end up as a quick snack for their larger clients. To try to prevent this, the wrasse advertise their role as cleaners via their distinctive and unique colour patterns.

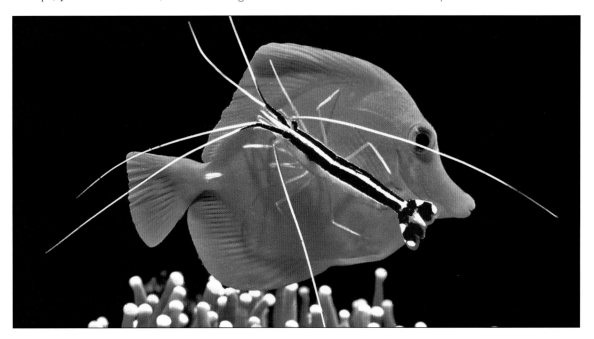

A symbiotic relationship

Probably the most famous example of a symbiotic ('living together') relationship on the coral reef – if not in the entire animal kingdom – is the remarkable relationship between clownfish and anemones.

Q: *How important is this relationship to the partner organisms?*

A: It seems that both organisms benefit considerably from the arrangement, but while only about 1% of all anemones host fish in this way, all species of clownfish in the wild are compelled to seek out an anemone. By living amongst an anemone's tentacles, the fish gain a protective refuge from predators, which are reluctant to expose themselves to a battery of stinging nematocysts. Clownfish are relatively poor swimmers and without the anemone will become the prey of larger fish sooner or later. The relationship is perhaps less important to the anemones, although some, like the bulb tentacle anemone (*Entacmaea quadricolor*) cannot live without

Below: A percula clownfish seeks the shelter of its home anemone. Few predators will risk the stings of the anemone to pursue the fish.

co-habiting fish in the wild. The clownfish provide protection for their anemones, driving off possible predators, such as butterflyfish.

Q: *What other benefits do clownfish provide for their anemones?*

A: Aquarists occasionally report instances where clownfish seem to feed their anemones, but it seems unlikely that this happens in nature, where the diet of clownfish is less likely to consist of large, messy chunks of food that might fall into the anemone's eager tentacles. The fish may, however, benefit their host by fanning them with water and keeping them free of parasites.

Q: *Can all clownfishes live with all anemones?*

A: There are something like 27 species of clownfish, but not all of these are able to live with the 11 anemones (out of around 1,000 species worldwide) that host fish. In fact, only the yellowtail clownfish (*Amphiprion clarkii*) is thought to occur naturally with all host anemones, while some clownfish are only found

Left: Blunt-headed wrasse have also developed immunity to the anemone's stings, allowing them to enjoy its protection.

in the wild with one anemone species. There are even a few other species of fish and inverts that live with anemones to a greater or lesser extent, including the blunt-headed wrasse (*Thalassoma amblycephalum*) and the porcelain anemone crab (*Neopetrolisthes ohshimai*).

Q: How are clownfish protected from the stinging cells of their host anemones?

A: Clownfish are protected from the stinging cells of their host anemone by a coating of protective mucus over their bodies. The fish are actually vulnerable to the anemone's toxins, but the mucus prevents the stinging cells from firing. However, whereas the yellowtail clownfish seems to have developed more or less permanent, general protection, most clownfish species have to acclimatise to a new anemone.

During this process, the fish start off by touching their ventral fins and belly area to the stinging tentacles of the anemone – and are stung in the process. Over a period of several hours, the fish become immune to the stings and can venture deeper into the anemone. Whether the protective mucus is produced by the fish itself, or is gathered from the anemone, or both, is unclear,

Below: Porcelain anemone crabs seek refuge in anemones and may attack its predators.

but it works by preventing the anemone from recognising the fish as a threat. In effect, the fish chemically mimics the anemone – and thus stops the stinging nematocysts from firing.

Q: How do clownfish choose their anemones?

A: If a fish chooses the wrong species of anemone when it settles, it could easily be killed. Juvenile clownfish are able to locate their anemones using chemical recognition of particular host species. Clownfish eggs are laid in close proximity to their host anemone and it seems likely that during this developmental stage, the embryonic fish may be imprinted with chemical cues from the anemone. Thus, when they select an anemone in later life, they choose the same species that their parents occupied.

Shrimps and gobies

Dramatic living arrangements between two completely different species are not confined to anemones and their clownfish lodgers. The relationship that sometimes occurs between shrimps and gobies is equally fascinating.

Q: How does the shrimp and goby relationship work?

A: Some species of shrimps and gobies have a living arrangement that benefits both. The animals cohabit in shared burrows, excavated from the sands of reef lagoons or among coral heads in sheltered areas. The shrimp is extremely active, digging out the burrow and keeping it clear of debris, while the goby stands guard at the burrow's entrance, looking out for approaching danger in the form of predators.

Q: What does each partner gain from the relationship?

A: The relationship seems to work because each of the partners has an Achilles heel that is compensated for by the other. The weakness of the shrimp is

its poor eyesight, which makes it a potentially easy meal for predators. On the other hand, the goby has excellent eyesight and is able to keep a lookout for danger on the shrimp's behalf, but is far less capable than its crustacean housemate of excavating its own burrow. It benefits from the protection that the shrimp's burrow provides. Both partners survive for longer with these living arrangements than they would alone.

Below: Steinitz's shrimp goby keeps a lookout while its shrimp burrow-mate shovels small bits of substrate out of their shared home.

Q: How does the goby warn the shrimp of impending danger?

A: If an inquisitive predator gets too close for comfort, the goby will respond by reversing into the burrow refuge. As it does so, it also communicates the danger to the shrimp by wiggling its tail as a warning. The shrimp picks up the warning through its antennae – whenever it leaves the burrow it keeps one of its feelers in constant contact with the fish, ready to pick up these warning messages and prepared at a moment's notice to take heed and duck into the hole.

Above: *The superior eyesight of Wheeler's shrimp goby* (Amblyeleotris wheeleri) *warns its cohabiting shrimp of any inquisitive predators.*

Q: Do gobies and shrimps have to live together?

A: Several species of shrimps and gobies live alongside one another in this way. Some are described as 'obligate' burrow sharers, meaning that they cannot live outside this symbiotic partnership; others are 'facultative' burrow sharers and can live independently, although the benefits of the arrangement mean that often they do live in alliance with their shrimp or fish partner. However, studies have shown that shrimps gain a far greater benefit from living with an obligate symbiont than with a facultative one. For example, when they live with the orangespotted goby *(Nes longus)*, an obligate partner, they can spend three times as long outside their burrow – meaning more digging and foraging time – than when they live with a facultative partner, such as the notchtongue goby *(Bathygobius curacao)*. This fish does not provide the shrimp with any special warning signals, other than a head-first dash into the burrow. Even so, the shrimps are able to spend longer outside the burrow when in association with a fish partner – even a poor one – than they could alone.

Q: How do gobies and shrimps find each other?

A: Long flat plains of sandy sea bed are extremely hazardous for small animals such as shrimps and gobies, so they need to find a partner quickly. Gobies use their eyesight to look out for shrimps, whilst the shrimps seek out partners by attuning to the fish's smell. Each is strongly attracted to the other, helping them locate and benefit each other with the mutual protection that their partnership provides.

Chapter 8

Battle of the sexes

Reef fishes are perhaps the most remarkable sexual strategists in the animal kingdom. Until relatively recently, their variety of lifestyles was unsuspected by biologists; it adds a fascinating extra dimension to the study of their behaviour.

Throughout the animal kingdom the interests of males and females are in conflict. For most species this means that males want to mate with as many different females as possible, whereas females try to avoid unwelcome advances and be more selective about their potential suitors. On the reef, the distinctions between male and female are often blurred; fish may be born male, switching to being female in later life or, more commonly, are born female and switch to being male.

Q: What's the reason for this conflict?

A: The reason for the so-called state of disharmony is at least partly due to a phenomenon known as anisogamy, which simply means 'different sized gametes'. Each sex produces cells – gametes – that contain genetic information. Male gametes are known as sperm, female sex cells are eggs. Fertilisation occurs when the two meet and fuse, which for most species of fish occurs in the water column. The great thing if you are male is that sperm cells are tiny in comparison to the eggs they fertilise, which means they require less energy to produce. What is more, males of most species can produce enough sperm cells to fertilise huge numbers of eggs. In other words, males have the capability to fertilise the eggs of tens, hundreds or even thousands of females if the chance arises. The more eggs he fertilises, the more genes he passes on, so the male strategy in the game of life is to court and cajole as many females as possible to mate with him. By contrast, females have to invest heavily in their eggs. Each one is packed with nutrients for the developing embryo and comes at a real cost. Females produce a finite number of eggs so it pays them to be choosy, to select the best father for their offspring, the one whose genes will give them the best chance of success in life.

Q: How unequal are the sexes in reality?

A: The inequality between the sexes is well illustrated by species such as cleaner wrasse, where a single male caters to a harem of females. The male can therefore

> ### The alternative battle of the sexes
>
> Although it is almost always male fish that compete amongst themselves for the attentions of females, there are exceptions to this rule. Because male seahorses brood their young in special pouches on their belly, this puts them is short supply and forces the females to compete for their mates.

manage to breed with several different partners, massively boosting his lifetime reproductive efforts in comparison to those of the females. Of course, the thing to remember is that for female wrasse, their chance may yet come to switch sides and become male themselves.

Q: *In what ways can we see the 'battle of the sexes' on the reef?*

A: As with any struggle, the two sides develop strategies. Females are picky about their partners, so males develop ways of attracting them. These include bright colours, unusual display behaviour patterns and ornamentation, such as the strange 'eyebrows', or more correctly 'cirri', of some male blennies. But all is not fair in love and war and many males have developed sneaky ways of circumventing female choice. Males also fight one another for the attentions of females. Although they are not limited by their physical ability to father offspring, their plans are sometimes limited by the presence of other males who are likely to have different ideas. Amongst species that provide parental care, males can be especially aggressive towards one another, as they need to defend

their territories, their mates and their young. Here, we will look at the sex war and at the fascinating ways in which fish have evolved as a consequence.

Below: Males of many fish species boast accessories that may be important in securing a mate. Male blennies, such as Salarias fasciatus, *often have cirri for this purpose.*

Which sex?

Reef fishes are faced with incredible pressures of competition because of the high densities under which they live and the ever-present danger of predation. As a result, they have evolved some incredible adaptations – none more so than the 'gender-bending' characteristics seen in some species. Certain species can be described as gonochorists – in other words, they have separate and fixed male and female sexes. However, the majority of reef fishes have taken the more flexible route and have become hermaphrodites, allowing them to 'have their cake and eat it'!

Q: What is an hermaphrodite?

A: The term hermaphrodite is applied to animals that possess both male and female sex organs in the same body, even if both are not necessarily functioning at the same time. The word itself comes from Hermaphroditus, a male character in Greek mythology, who was fused with a nymph to create an individual with the traits of both sexes.

Hermaphroditism is extremely rare in vertebrates, most of which are gonochorists.

Q: What's the benefit to being an hermaphrodite?

A: Changing sex allows fish to maximise their chances of passing on their genes. This is especially important for coral reef fish because their opportunities may be extremely limited by low life expectancy and by the difficulties in obtaining a territory – often a prerequisite for breeding males. In these circumstances, breeding opportunities for young and small males are almost non-existent, a difficulty they may overcome by spending the first part of their lives as females. If members of your own species are spread out and there is a great deal of danger involved in spending large amounts of time searching one out, it is worthwhile keeping open your sexual options. This is exactly what some juvenile coral gobies do; when they find a single, adult goby, they note which sex it is and develop into the opposite one.

Q: What are the different kinds of hermaphrodite?

A: Hermaphrodites can be divided into simultaneous hermaphrodites, who function

Below: Centropyge ferrugatus *is capable of switching not only from female to male, but apparently back again, making finding a mate on the reef considerably easier.*

Right: The black hamlet (Hypoplectrus nigricans) is a simultaneous hermaphrodite. Pairs change roles during spawning, taking turns to be male and female.

roles and, happily, this is exactly what happens in practice. First, the 'female' partner produces a package of eggs for the 'male' to fertilise and then they switch roles back and forth repeatedly. However, it is important for the first female-acting fish not to produce all her eggs at once. If she did, the male-acting fish could simply fertilise them all and then cheat on his side of the bargain by disappearing. By producing only a few eggs at a time, each fish makes sure that if it is cheated, the costs are not too high.

as both male and female at the same time, and sequential hermaphrodites, who start life as one sex and then change at a later period into the opposite sex. The first strategy is rare, although it is now clear that some fish, such as the rusty dwarf angel, that were thought to be sequential hermaphrodites are actually capable of switching back to their original gender.

than sperm. To split the costs fairly, a spawning pair should theoretically alternate between fulfilling the male and female

Making up your mind

Recent research has shown that fish, unusually amongst higher animals, keep their options open with regard to gender, committing to be male or female in response to the presence or absence of potential mates.

Q: Are there any reef fish that are simultaneous hermaphrodites?

A: Although rare, there are some species of grouper that function as both male and female at the same time. The black hamlet fish is one such species. A problem faced by these fish face when they spawn is that, as we have seen (page 160), eggs are more costly to produce

A young goby with no clearly determined sex encounters a mature male of its own species.

The mature male starts to court the newcomer.

The opportunity to mate with an established male causes the juvenile to develop into a female.

Protogyny – ladies first

Protogyny – where fish spend the first part of their lives as females before becoming males when they are older and larger – is by far the most common form of sequential hermaphroditism seen among coral reef fishes. Protogyny is seen amongst species of wrasse, parrotfish and groupers, as well as in some damsels, angels and gobies. As a result, most of the small fish seen on the coral reef are females.

Above: Parrotfish and wrasses spend the first part of their adult lives as females. If they survive and grow, they will become males.

Q: *What are the benefits of protogyny?*

A: The different gender strategies that coral reef fish follow are all about one thing – maximising the number of offspring they can produce during their lives. For the most part, small males do not get a look in on the reef; in order to mate they may often need a territory, and tiddlers find it tough to get a territory. Therefore, during this early part of their adult lives it is beneficial to breed as a female, because the alternative is not to breed at all. While living as females they can choose to breed with the best

male, thereby securing the best genes for their offspring. If they manage to survive and grow to a good size, they may then switch to being a male themselves and, in some species, adopt their own harem of females, again boosting their reproductive capabilities.

Q: *What decides when protogynous fish change sex?*

A: The presence of a male is sometimes enough to prevent females from switching sex and becoming male themselves, although occasionally this has to be backed up by direct

aggression from a male. For example, male cleaner wrasse (*Labroides dimidiatus*) save most of their aggression for the largest females in their harem, because these are ones on the cusp of becoming male. This bullying appears to affect the females at a hormonal level, keeping the door to becoming male firmly shut. However, if the male disappears, one of these females can change its gender within a matter of days. The problem for the developing male is that he could now lose his newly inherited harem, who all have to wait until he changes physiologically and is able to fertilise their eggs. To try to prevent this, the largest female in a group of tail-spot wrasse (*Halichoeres melanurus*) starts to behave like a male as little as 20 minutes after the disappearance of the dominant male, even to the point of simulating spawning with the females. However, if the male reappears, the thwarted female rapidly reassumes her former role. In fact, there is evidence from studies on dwarf angelfish to suggest that if a breeding male is bullied enough by another male, he will revert to his old female role.

Q: *What are primary and secondary males?*

A: If things were not already complicated enough, it seems that protogynous fish give rise to two different kinds of males. Fish that are born female and later turn into males are known as secondary males. But there is another small group of fish that seem to be born as males and remain male throughout their lives and these are known as primary males. In some species, such as the blue-barred parrotfish (*Scarus ghobban*), primary males advertise their masculinity through bright colours. On the other hand, some wrasse are more sneaky and despite being male, look like the more dull-coloured females. This allows them to sneak into the territories of larger males and fertilise the eggs of the females with whom they spawn clandestinely.

Changing places on the reef

Many reef fish species spend their early life as females, only becoming male as they grow and become socially dominant. But existing males fight this change, preferring that female mates stay female.

If the dominant male goes missing, some females start to switch sexes and fill the male role.

But if the male returns, he will block this change by acting aggressively towards the changeling.

In some species, newly changed males masquerade as females, sneakily mating under the nose of the unsuspecting dominant male.

Protandry – little boys to big girls

The opposite strategy to protogyny is known as protandry. In this case, fish start out as male before changing at some later point in life to being female. Although less common than protogyny, there are several protandrous fish, including scorpionfish, some bream, snapper and bass species and, most famously of all, clownfish.

Q: What are the benefits to protandry?

A: Given the way that large, aggressive males defend their territories on the reef, the benefits of protogyny are quite easy to understand. How switching to being female can benefit a fish as it grows is sometimes less obvious. Whereas males are capable of fertilising huge numbers of eggs regardless of their size, females are really limited by their size in their capacity to produce eggs. Because of this, many protogynous species breed in harems – one male mates with several females. But large females are able to produce more eggs than smaller ones and this is the most important factor in

protandry; one large female can produce as many eggs as several small females. Therefore, if males do not have to fight to establish a territory and gain mating rights, then protandry makes sense.

Q: What decides when protandrous fish change sex?

A: As with protogynous fish, the status quo is often maintained by aggression. For example, female clownfish can be twice

or even three times the size of their mates and their aggressive dominance of the males is what prevents the latter becoming female. The dominance hierarchy within the group of males at an anemone is also important in deciding who gets to become female. Studies on clownfish have shown that if two lone males cohabit an anemone, it is the bossy one that develops into a female. In the wild, if a female disappears or is taken by a predator, the most dominant

Clownfish society

Amongst fish that change sex during their lives, the typical pattern is to start as a female and become male. Clownfish, however, buck this trend.

1 *A group of clownfish – one large female and a handful of small males – occupy a home anemone.*

2 *If the female disappears, the largest and most dominant male will start to change into a female.*

male changes sex and takes her place at the top of the pecking order. The second-ranked male then moves up in the hierarchy and becomes the top-ranked, breeding male. In these species, the female very often enforces a monogamous existence on her subordinate partner, refusing to tolerate the presence of other females at the anemone and only breeding with the dominant male.

Q: Do males always change to become female when a vacancy occurs?

A: Changing sex is not as simple as flipping a switch. A fish has to adopt different behaviour patterns and undergo physiological changes that can take anything up to two or three

3 *The new female becomes head of the group, occupying the role left by the previous female.*

months. While this is going on, the fish is out of the game as far as reproduction is concerned. Two months is a long time in a fish's life; it can miss out on mating opportunities — even missing the rest of the breeding season, which could represent a huge cost. As a result, males sometimes put their changes on hold and seek out ready-made mates instead. If the resident

Above: As with other clownfish species, the female Premnas biaculeatus *is far larger than her mate. Her size allows her to lay larger broods of eggs than if she was as small as the male.*

female disappears outside the breeding season the change is much more likely to happen rapidly, because the male is less likely to miss out at this time.

Vive la difference!

Of course, not all reef fishes are hermaphrodites. Some species show fixed gender patterns from birth, others take a little longer to choose and this is where the whole situation becomes blurred. For scientists, determining which fish do what when it comes to gender-bending is far from simple. Just when things seem to be decided, the fish produce a new surprise.

Q: *Which reef fishes have fixed genders?*

A: Although new discoveries continually throw up surprises in the unusual world of reef fish life history strategies, there are still several species where individual fish are thought to remain as either males or females throughout their lives. These include butterflyfish, firefish, surgeons and tangs, pufferfish, rabbitfish, jawfish, cardinalfish, seahorses and some angelfish. To complicate matters, there is another group of fish, including some gobies, sometimes referred to as 'secondary

gonochorists' and their sex is effectively decided by their social environment.

Q: *What's the benefit to having separate sexes?*

A: There are so many advantages to reef fish in being hermaphroditic, it seems strange that some fish tie themselves down to one or other sex for life. The reasons for this are subject to a great deal of speculation but one suggestion involves the costs of switching sex. As well as the physiological costs involved in adapting the body to a new gender, individuals can also miss

Above: Chaetodon auriga *does not change sex during its life. It has this in common with most vertebrates, but is unlike many of the fish that it shares the reef with.*

out on mating opportunities during their changeover and even for a period afterwards. For example, when some wrasse switch to being males they then have to fight for a territory of their own. If they fail to secure one quickly, they can be left in limbo for an important part of their reproductive life. Other possible reasons for maintaining sex differences in some species could include the need for males in species such as cardinalfish and seahorses to develop pouch-like structures to carry their developing eggs.

Q: How do secondary gonochorists decide which sex to be?

A: Keeping your options open is a useful strategy, especially if life is full of danger and fraught with difficulty. These are the conditions under which small fish such as the broad-barred goby *(Gobiodon histrio)* live. These and related species form close associations with branching corals for protection. However, only pairs are able to establish and defend a really good coral territory, so juveniles in the area must remain patient until an opening occurs – caused by the death of one of the pair – or they must risk their lives to search out a lone adult of their own. Either way, when that happens, the juvenile fish cannot take the risk that the newly located adult is the wrong sex, so it simply waits to find out the adult's sex and then matures into the opposite one.

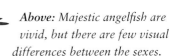

Above: Majestic angelfish are vivid, but there are few visual differences between the sexes.

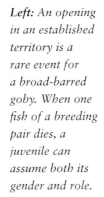

Left: An opening in an established territory is a rare event for a broad-barred goby. When one fish of a breeding pair dies, a juvenile can assume both its gender and role.

Above: Seahorses have clearly defined sexes and sex roles. Females produce the eggs, but it is the males that brood them.

Dressed to thrill

Reproduction – passing on genes to the next generation – is the ultimate goal of every animal on the reef. The way in which the different sexes approach this is very different, even for fish that grew up as a member of the opposite sex. Basically, males can afford to be free and easy because they are capable of mating with any number of females. By contrast, females are choosy because their mating opportunities are constrained by their ability to produce eggs. They cannot mate nearly as often as males, so when they do they must pick out the best possible partner. This fundamental difference in motivation between males and females is responsible for some of the bright coloration and amazing behaviour seen in reef fishes, and for the sexual dimorphism – differences in appearance between the sexes – apparent in some species.

Right: The male Genicanthus watanabei *has distinctive striped livery. Females are pale blue and lack the distinctive bars.*

Q: *Are the colour patterns of male fish used to display to females?*

A: Many different coral reef fishes show sexual dichromatism – colour differences between the genders. It functions both as a warning signal to other males and as an advertisement to females. Male sergeant major damselfish turn blue prior to mating, signalling their availability to females. Other species maintain fairly consistent levels of adult colour-pattern differences between the genders. For example, male sunrise dottybacks are a dramatic vivid bright blue with a yellow trim, while the females are a far more sober beige colour. Sexual dichromatism is also a feature in some kinds of angelfish, such as the swallowtail angelfishes (*Genicanthus* spp.), but not in

other members of the same family. One of the reasons for this lack of consistency stems from the fact that females can assess a range of different characteristics (morphologies) in males. Whereas some use colour, others rely on other indicators of male quality. As well as this, sexual dichromatism – or the lack of it – is not just about attracting females, but relates in a much more general way to the social behaviour of the species in question.

Q: *What male morphologies are used for attracting a mate?*

A: Perhaps the most obvious of these is size. In many species males are larger than females, but this is scarcely surprising in the case of protogynous fish that become male only when they grow large. Size is also mixed up with competition between males for territory space, so a female that picks a large male is not necessarily choosing on the basis of his size, but rather assessing his dominance status or his territory. Female wrasse or basslets that live in harems may be content to mate with the dominant male because simply by maintaining a territory and a harem (and having worked 'his' way to the top as a 'her' – remember these are protogynous fish) he must be a good-quality mate. These males also develop certain sexually dimorphic traits: male wrasse often have elongated pelvic fins, while male lyretail anthias also develop extended dorsal fin

rays. These not only mark out their sex to females, but can also be displayed to a male rival to warn him off. Males of many blenny species show marked morphological differences from their mates, including larger cirri and taller dorsal fins, which may relate to a female blenny's idea of what makes for a sexy partner.

Above: Male sergeant majors become flushed with blue during the mating season, helping them to attract potential mates.

Below: As individual Pseudanthias squamipinnis *age, they switch gender, and the plain yellow female becomes a much showier multicoloured male.*

Don't judge by appearances

When males attempt to attract females to mate with them, colour patterns and other physical characteristics may often be important but they are not everything. A male may be extremely handsome in fish terms, but in most cases, he still has a way to go before convincing a sceptical female to part with her costly cargo of eggs. Courtship on the coral reef can often be extremely energetic. Males may have many competitors nearby, so they have to do something really special to gain a female's attention and they may use visual signals, smells and sounds to achieve this.

Q: What behavioural displays do males use?

A: Male courtship displays are extremely important in many coral reef fish species. Territorial fish are often constrained to remain near their hard-fought patch, otherwise they may lose it. This means that they must signal to females to encourage them to visit. The male alamo'o (Lentipes concolor) sits on a rock and waves its bright yellow tail

towards females for this reason. Damselfish displays have been extensively studied. Males roll their bodies and then dive towards the substrate in front of the female, before nudging and nuzzling at her belly with their snout. Once the male has gained his amour's attention, he attempts to lead her towards his nest site, where he may continue to quiver and tilt his body towards the oviposition site. Damselfish are far from the only males that try to dance their way into a female's affections; angelfish often have complex, ritualised sexual displays. These may involve the male nuzzling the female's flank as an encouragement to her to spawn, or quivering his entire body. Male angelfish also use their tail fins in display, fluttering them in the female's face. Often, males of many species will begin their displays when they see a female, but frill-fin gobies start to display even if they can only smell and not see a mate.

Q: Are males' territories important to a female's choice?

A: A male fish's territory is an extremely good indicator of his quality – there is a linear relationship between

Below: Courtship is often a ritualised affair. Here, a pair of Chaetodon semilarvatus *begin to size up one another.*

by comparing territories, they also assess the location of the territory and the likelihood of attack by a predator. If he wants to attract a female to spawn there, a male triple-fin blenny's territory must be able to provide the developing eggs with shelter, both from predators and

from prevailing currents. Competition for territories that include these desirable features is intense. The very intensity of the competition usually results in the best male taking possession, so the female blenny gets everything she wants – a sexy male and a safe nest.

his attributes and those of his territory – so it makes sense for a female to pick him on the basis of this. In fact, in these cases, females not only pick a mate

Q: *What other displays do males use?*

A: If colourful displays, courtship or territory quality do not quite convince a female, the males of some species start to serenade them as well. At various stages of their courtship, male damselfish produce distinct and different sounds to accompany their energetic rolls, pitches and dives. Playback experiments using underwater speakers have shown that females prefer the songs of larger – presumably more dominant – males. Toadfish take a rather more relaxed approach; they just sit still and 'sing' to attract females, rather like toads themselves do. Butterflyfish have extremely advanced sound-producing and receiving abilities, and pair-forming species are thought to produce clicks both in courtship and in long-term recognition between members of a monogamous pair.

Speaking fish

Fish displays convey crucial information, never more so than in the breeding season as they court one another. At this time of year, fish exhibit their most dramatic and sometimes baffling behaviour.

Signals and displays

Breeding is such an important part of a fish's life, that it is of little surprise that males devote so much effort and energy to courtship, or that females make such careful, considered mate choice judgements. But exactly how much effort do males put in – what does courtship cost them? How do females weigh up all the different males and all their different criteria? And what happens to the males who cannot attract partners?

Q: Are male sexual signals costly?

A: Although standing out from the crowd is a great tactic for attracting the attention of impressionable females, it also brings males to the attention of hungry predators and this is clearly a major cost to male courtship. To try to restrict their risk, both pipefish and gobies scale down their displays when a predator is around. The bright colours exhibited by some males may also bring them to the attention of predators; for example, fairy wrasse (Cirrhilabrus sp.) are far more colourful as males than

as females and may be more conspicuous to predators. The bright colours may also attract aggression from other males, which is another cost to advertising yourself. Male flasher wrasse have come up with an ingenious solution to this problem – they turn on their amazing neon blue courtship colours only in the latter stages of courtship and turn them off again immediately after spawning. On top of being conspicuous, the physiological effort in maintaining vivid colours or performing

elaborate courtship displays can be exhausting for males. So much so, in fact, that only the healthiest males can put on a really good show. This, of course, helps the females to make their choice.

Q: Which is the most important of a male's characteristics for attracting a mate?

A: It is easy to understand that if a female is confronted with a large, brightly coloured male and a small, drab one, she is likely to

Above: The male flasher wrasse (Paracheilinus filamentosus) *is attractively coloured at all times, but when courting (left) he produces a brilliant fin-flashing display.*

choose the former. But in the real world, a female is confronted by many different, sometimes conflicting, male characteristics and it can be hard for us to work out the factors weighing most heavily in her decision. However, a remarkable study on tail-spot wrasse did manage to separate these out, reporting that although body size is important in deciding which male gets which territory, the females actually chose their male on the basis of the conspicuousness of his colour, especially the yellow spot that the male carries at the base of its pectoral fin. Meanwhile, female beaugregory damsels place a high degree of importance on both the males' yellow breeding garb and on the frequency with which they perform the stereotypical dives in their courtship.

Q: *How can other males compete?*

A: If males cannot gain access to females by fair means, they may resort to devious tactics. These usually involve shadowing dominant males in order to intercept some females as they approach his territory and cajole them into spawning with them instead of the dominant. A variation on this theme occurs when, instead of intercepting the

Putting on a show

When it comes to dramatic and colourful courtship displays, male reef fishes must have what the watching female is looking for.

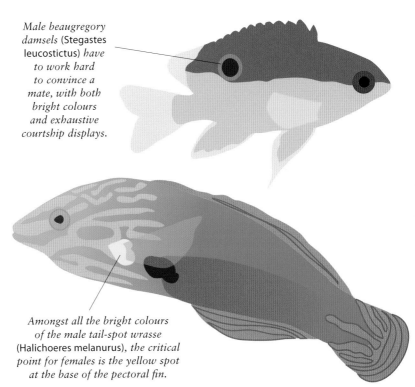

Male beaugregory damsels (Stegastes leucostictus) *have to work hard to convince a mate, with both bright colours and exhaustive courtship displays.*

Amongst all the bright colours of the male tail-spot wrasse (Halichoeres melanurus), *the critical point for females is the yellow spot at the base of the pectoral fin.*

females themselves, the sneaky males hang around, closely watching the courtship of the dominant male. When the pair ascend to spawn, the shadowing males dash in with them and, if they time it right, fertilise some eggs for themselves. This behaviour is sometimes called 'streaking' and is commonly seen in some protogynous species, such as blueheaded

wrasse and bluebanded gobies, where some of the population are born as males and remain so throughout their lives. These so-called primary males look almost exactly like females and use this fact to gain access to the dominant male's territory. By the time the irate territory holder realises that he has been duped it is too late to do any more than chase off the intruder.

Choosy females

The choices made by females exert huge influence on the behaviour and appearance of males throughout the animal kingdom. As we have seen, male reef fishes almost fall over themselves to grab the attention of a female, even resorting to underhand tactics if honesty fails to pay. The picky female and her male of choice thereby pass on their genes to the next generation and, if the female has chosen well, the genetic package that their offspring inherit will stand them in good stead for their own lives.

Q: *What do females gain from being picky?*

A: A female selects her mate carefully for the sake of the next generation. If she can pick a really top class mate, their offspring are likely to have correspondingly good genes and, as a result, be more successful in their own life. So by picking the best possible male, a female gives herself the best possible chance of genetic immortality throughout subsequent generations. There are benefits in the short term as well. For example, the male

Above: Male yellowmargin triggerfish carefully construct and defend a nesting territory, hoping that a female will choose them.

bicolour damsels that are most active in their courtship displays are also the best at guarding their eggs from the many predators that threaten nests. So courtship displays and the colour patterns of the male all give the female clues about his quality. Only the best males can afford to invest in energetically expensive courtships and only the healthiest

and most robust of them can produce vivid colours or win the best territories. A good male is one of life's winners.

Q: *Are females all equally choosy?*

A: Some females are extremely picky. For example, female mandarins lay a great deal of emphasis on the colour pattern of prospective suitors, so much so that some females may prefer not to mate at all than to compromise their high standards.

In the yellowmargin triggerfish (*Pseudobalistes flavimarginatus*), the males migrate to a long-standing, traditional mating ground, where each fights to gain control of a small territory containing a spawning site and awaits the arrival of the females. It takes several days for the females to arrive, but when they do, they take great care in selecting a mate, assessing both the male and his territory before deciding and laying eggs. The pair then share the responsibility of caring for their brood until they hatch. At the other end of the scale are fish that breed in large spawning aggregations, such as some surgeonfish and snappers. For them there is little courtship and equally little difference between the sexes. The female has comparatively little choice over who fathers her offspring and there is little advantage to the male in being showy – better for him that he should be quick instead! Female crabs, too, have far less say in whom they mate with. Crabs can only mate once the female has moulted, but after shedding her hard shell she is extremely vulnerable for several hours or even days and would find it extremely difficult to resist the overtures of a male. In some cases, a male can sense the presence of a female who is about to moult and guards her aggressively from other suitors before and even after mating.

Below: In common with many crab species, male blue swimming crabs (Portunus pelagicus) *can detect when a female is about to moult and therefore ready to mate.*

Choosy females

Choosing the right mate is so important to female reef fishes that they are prepared to make considerable sacrifices to ensure that they end up with the best possible one. Recent research has shown that females use all sorts of different criteria when choosing. Rather than simply falling for the first male with a half-decent courtship display, females pay close attention to the choices of other females to try to ensure that they end up with the perfect father for their offspring.

Q: Is it costly to be choosy?

A: To find the best male, females of some species must go farther afield than their immediate surroundings. A study on red-lip blennies showed that females would travel as much as 12 metres from their own feeding territories in search of a good mate – quite a distance for a small and vulnerable fish. Those that ventured furthest did indeed manage to get the best males, but their travels carried the cost to them of being attacked by the damselfish whose territories they

were forced to cross on the way. In other species, going in search of a good mate can expose a choosy female to predation risk on top of the energetic expense of increased travel distance. These reasons all suggest that females that live in harems have it comparatively easy. There may also be a further cost to females in selecting the so-called best males: for example, popular male blueheaded wrasse are actually less successful at fertilising eggs than their less-favoured brethren. The popular males are the most attractive, which puts them in high demand with the females. For this reason, they conserve resources and in doing so fertilise the eggs of many different females. The cost to each female is a lower fertility rate, but the

benefit is that her offspring get the best genes.

Q: How else can females decide who may be the best mate?

A: One way for a female to make sure that she is getting the best possible male is to watch other females to see who they choose. Females of a number of different species have been shown to seek out and lay their eggs in nests that already contain eggs. Female blennies are

Below: Despite the risks of travelling across unfamiliar territory, distance is no object to a female red-lip blenny (Ophioblennius atlanticus) when she looks for a top-class mate.

known to do this, but they do exercise some restraint. If a nest has too many eggs already, the developing embryos are likely to be using up a large amount of oxygen. Therefore, the female blennies prefer nests containing some – but not too many – eggs. Female Garibaldi damsels take this a step further and prefer nests with young eggs in. If older eggs are in the nest, there is a risk that the male may reduce his brood care once these hatch,

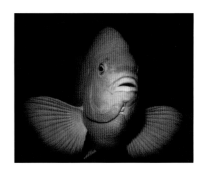

Mate choice copying

1 *Female coral reef fishes take a close interest in the behaviour of other females and often copy their mate and spawning choices.*

2 *If a male has been chosen before, it seems to reinforce his appeal to other females, who are then more willing to mate with him.*

3 *The most successful males can end up guarding a brood of eggs produced by several different females.*

*Above: Female Garibaldi damselfishes (*Hypsypops rubicundus*) are strongly influenced by the choices of other females.*

leaving remaining, late-hatching eggs unguarded. Males will even eat old eggs in their own nests to make sure they do not miss out when a new female comes calling. After they pick a nest, female bicolour damsels tend to return time after time to spawn with the same male. But if the male's nest is targeted by a persistent egg-predator, such as a brittle-star, the females rapidly switch to a new partner. Female white-belly damselfish *(Amblyglyphidodon leucogaster)* seem to take note of which males other females in the population spawn with and use this information when they decide for themselves. They can remember who is who in the dating game for considerable periods and this allows them to make an informed choice to spawn with the local hotshot.

Chapter 9
Mating systems

The question of how best to make sure that your offspring survive to carry on the genetic line is a crucial one for all animals, but it is also a question with many different possible solutions, as reef animals clearly demonstrate.

The high densities of animals on coral reefs mean that the chances of survival of any eggs that remain in the locale are extremely low. Reef animals may either produce buoyant eggs that float to safety on offshore currents or they may lay demersal eggs and invest in parental care. This increases the chances of survival in early life by keeping their predators at bay. Between these two extremes, reef animals show an amazing variety of reproductive strategies.

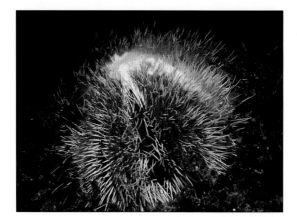

Left: Animals such as sea urchins broadcast large numbers of eggs into the water in the hope that a few will survive to adulthood.

Q: Why do species that live in the same habitat use so many different reproductive strategies?

A: The important thing to remember is that what may work for one species may not work for another. Only a tiny fraction of the offspring are likely to survive in any situation, but anything that gives the young

an edge will be favoured by evolution. In large, long-living fish, egg-guarding is relatively rare. The majority of egg-guarding amongst reef fishes is carried out by species measuring less than 10cm long. Smaller species are only able to produce a limited number of eggs, so it may pay them to invest in parental care. By contrast, larger fish can turn out enormous numbers of eggs over the course of their lives and have a good chance of producing surviving offspring without having to provide parental care.

Q: What other factors decide which species follow which strategy?

A: Sessile invertebrates, such as corals, are clearly not free to move around in search of a mate or to defend their young. This means they have to use a lottery system of releasing millions of gametes into the environment in the hope that some will survive. Mobile invertebrates and fish have more options, but it is usually only those that spend their lives within a limited home range, and that live in close contact with the reef itself, that have the option to remain in one place to guard eggs.

Q: *Why do some fish spawn in groups, while others form pair bonds?*

A: The butterflyfish family exhibits a range of reproductive strategies along these lines, which relate in turn to their diet. For example, planktivorous species, such as the lemon butterflyfish (*Chaetodon milliaris*), tend to

live and spawn in groups. This is because plankton is a patchy and unpredictable food source and the fish that feed on them must move around the reef in shoals to search for food. By contrast, fish that browse on coral, such as the pebbled butterflyfish (*Chaetodon multicinctus*), feed on a predictable food source. They are able to defend food territories and to stay in one area; males defend territories from other males, while allowing a female access to their territory. By undertaking

most of the territorial defensive duties themselves, the males allow the females to increase their food intake, which in turn increases the number of eggs they can produce. This reciprocal arrangement between the males and females leads to long-term pair bonds.

Below: Species such as bigfin reef squids (Sepioteutis lessoniana) *lay their eggs in large sticky clutches. The sheer number of simultaneous spawnings means that at least some of the embryos will survive.*

Spawning corals

It is sometimes easy to forget that the huge inert structures upon and around which fish and inverts teem are themselves alive. But the incredible sight of a spawning reef turning the water milky white and drawing in feeding animals, from tiny crustaceans to the colossal whale sharks, acts as a reminder that the corals are living animals.

Q: *How do corals reproduce?*

A: Corals can reproduce in one of two ways: asexually or sexually. In the first case, each polyp produces a miniature clone of itself by budding. A new individual appears as a bud on an existing polyp and gradually grows before splitting away to live independently. In this way, colonies of corals can grow comparatively quickly. Some corals also breed asexually by producing miniature clonal larvae, which they release into the water to establish new colonies. However, corals can also reproduce sexually, most often through spectacular mass spawning events, where multitudes of corals simultaneously release their eggs and sperm into the water.

Above: Coral reproduction needs to be closely co-ordinated to avoid wasting precious resources. When conditions are just right a mass spawning of corals is triggered.

Reef reproduction

At certain times of the year, corals produce huge numbers of eggs. The few that survive to settle, form new coral colonies on the reef.

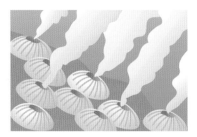

1 *Environmental triggers cause the corals to release their gametes en masse into the open water.*

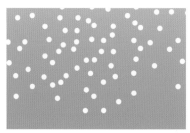

2 *Eggs and sperm fuse in the water column, forming embryonic corals that drift in the plankton.*

3 *The majority of the gametes and fertilised eggs become food for reef animals, such as this fanworm.*

Q: *How do the different corals fertilise one another?*

A: Coral colonies start to breed once they reach sexual maturity. This can take several years for some of the slower-growing corals, such as brain corals, although soft corals grow more quickly and mature earlier. Coral eggs can be fertilised by mixing with sperm in the water column, or within a female polyp. Most species, known as broadcasters, reproduce by the first method. The other breeding strategy is known as brooding. Instead of sperm and eggs mixing freely in the water, fertilisation takes place in the comparative safety of a female polyp. In both cases, once the fertilised eggs hatch, the larvae drift amongst the plankton for anything up to a month before settling onto the reef and metamorphosing into polyps. However, competition for space is intense and most of the newly settled polyps fail to establish themselves, falling prey to innumerable predators or being excluded by aggressive mature corals. If they do succeed in laying down a limestone skeleton, they can start to grow rapidly, first by budding and then ultimately by reaching maturity and breeding sexually, so completing the life cycle.

Q: *What triggers spawning in corals?*

A: Sessile organisms cannot go out to hunt for a mate, but nor can they afford simply to release precious gametes into the open waters of the reef, where they would quickly become food for the many fish and invertebrates. Mass spawning provides one highly effective means of overcoming their predators. In essence, by a concerted spawning effort, the corals can produce so many offspring that the gathered hordes of predators are swamped. But for this to work the corals must synchronise their breeding efforts. Many species also rely on strong currents to disperse their young, so they breed during spring tides when the tidal range and the currents are at their greatest. Changes in the tidal patterns may trigger the corals to spawn, along with seasonal fluctuations in temperature. Some species are also thought to be stimulated by the presence in the water of breeding pheromones from other sessile reef organisms.

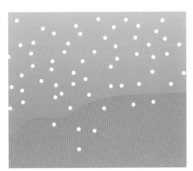

4 *The survivors drift towards a stable substrate, where they may take a hold and establish.*

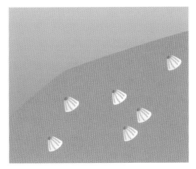

5 *New and tiny coral polyps develop on the vastness of the reef. Even now, survival is rare.*

6 *Gradually, the new colony develops and the single polyps begin to reproduce and spread.*

Invertebrate reproduction

There are almost as many reproductive strategies amongst the reef invertebrates as there are species. Some of the more simple animals produce clones of themselves by asexual budding, whereas others are amongst the most dedicated animal parents on the planet. Although there is a temptation to think of breeding tactics such as parental care as 'the best' – perhaps because they are most similar to our own – all the strategies used by reef species are successful in their own context.

Above: Anemones, such as this Nemanthus *sp. can spread by asexual budding. Each tiny new clone can eventually grow to be the size of its parent.*

Q: *Apart from corals, which other reef invertebrate species can reproduce asexually?*

A: Related species, such as anemones, often use asexual reproduction when conditions are at their most ideal, splitting in two or simply budding to form an offspring that is a clone of the parent. Many starfish follow a similar pattern. In the multipore starfish (*Linckia multifora*), the animal holds onto the substrate while one arm moves away and tears itself from the rest. Both

parts gradually regenerate to look like the original parent.

Q: *Which inverts broadcast their eggs?*

A: For sessile, or slow-moving, invertebrates, a release of gametes into the water column is usually essential for the animals to reproduce. Even those that are capable of asexual reproduction usually reproduce in this way once they reach

maturity. Many bivalve molluscs, including clams, shed their eggs to be fertilised in open water, as do tropical urchins and sponges. Some starfish also reproduce in this way, seeking high spots on the reef and even raising portions of their body above the substrate to release their eggs. Some species of polychaete worms reproduce by apparently shedding the posterior half of their bodies. This epitoke, as it is called, is in fact a sac full of gametes that wriggles its way through the water. Mass spawning events of these worms are triggered at certain times of year and the sea becomes a mass of writhing white epitokes, which

Left: Inverts, such as this peacock mantis shrimp (Odontodactylus scyllarus), make excellent parents, carrying their eggs and protecting them from opportunistic predators.

are prized as a food source by many human societies. A few hours later, the sacs rupture at the surface, releasing gametes so that fertilisation can occur and the embryonic worms can drop to the substrate to begin life.

Q: Which are the best parents amongst the reef invertebrates?

A: Many marine snails lay their eggs in clumps, protected by a jelly that also later serves to feed the newly hatched young. Crustaceans, such as shrimps and some crabs, carry their fertilised eggs around with them, usually underneath their abdomens where they are at least as safe as their parent. But the prize for the most dedicated parent amongst the invertebrates probably goes to the octopus. Females either

lay their eggs in nests or carry them around with them. During their long development, the female octopus guards the eggs determinedly from any potential threat, cleaning them and passing currents of water over them to provide a good supply of oxygen.

In many cases, the guarding parent does not even eat throughout this process and dies soon after the young hatch.

Below: Gymnodoris ceylonica embryos develop inside a jelly before eating their way to freedom.

Broadcast spawning in fish

Broadcast, or scatter, spawning is probably the most common tactic for reproduction amongst fish – around 80% of tropical marine fish spawn in this way. This hints at its effectiveness; if no fry ever survived, then scatter spawning would very quickly be abandoned as a strategy. That said, only a fraction of one percent of all the eggs produced will ever grow to adulthood, but the more eggs the parents produce, the greater their chances of winning in the fish lottery. In this case, the prize is a place for their offspring in the next generation.

Q: How does broadcast spawning work?

A: Whether the fish gather at some traditional mating ground or the females visit males inside their territories, most broadcast-spawning species spawn in the same way, casting thousands or even millions of eggs to the currents. The pair gather together before darting away from the reef to release their eggs.

Q: Why do spawning pairs rise up into the water column at the point of spawning?

A: The chief reason for the mating ascent is thought to be to enable breeding pairs to release their eggs away from the hordes of egg predators and into the water currents that will carry them away from the reef. Exactly how far they rise during the mating ascent varies between species; smaller species are understandably wary of predators, so keep their ascent

The mating ascent

Some tropical marine fish species gather into large spawning aggregations. Occasionally, fish leave the shoal and burst upwards in a mating ascent.

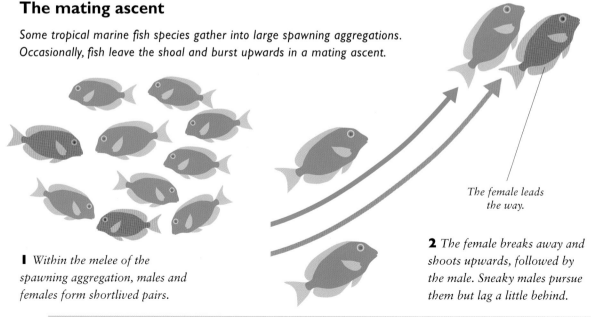

The female leads the way.

1 *Within the melee of the spawning aggregation, males and females form shortlived pairs.*

2 *The female breaks away and shoots upwards, followed by the male. Sneaky males pursue them but lag a little behind.*

to a minimum. Larger species, such as regal angels, may rise several metres away from the reef. There is little privacy on the reef and breeding pairs of fish are very often joined by other fish, especially unwelcome males. The mating ascent is one means by which the dominant male can restrict the success of these satellite males. This is best achieved by making the ascent itself as fast as possible and catching those other males off guard. Pairs of striped parrotfish (*Scarus iseri*) burst upwards in their mating ascent at speeds of anything up to 40km per hour. At the top of the ascent, after spawning, it is common for males from many different species to flick their tails upwards, creating a vortex that carries the sperm and eggs further upwards, away from competing males and hungry egg-predators alike.

Q: How can fish increase the chances of survival for their offspring?

A: The mortality rate of the vulnerable eggs is extremely high. On average, around a third are eaten in the first 24 hours of their life and much of this predation occurs before the eggs have even drifted from the reef. The mating ascent is one means of restricting these losses; as they rise, pairs of some species change their trajectories to throw the predators off the trail. Some parents even remain to attack any predators bold enough to feed close to them, though such

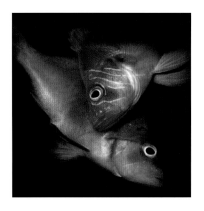

Above: Hypoplectrus puella *ascend to spawn as dusk approaches. The pair clasp each other with their tail around the other's nose.*

parental care is rare. In most cases, the fish spawn within a short period either side of dusk, which is another means of giving the eggs a fair chance of avoiding predation. In nearly all broadcast-spawning species, the eggs hatch extremely quickly, some in less than a day. Although still highly vulnerable, newly hatched larvae at least have the defence of mobility. Some species, such as scorpionfish and lionfish, produce packets of several thousand eggs, bound together in a jellylike ball that stays together until the eggs are close to hatching. These floating egg packets defeat the efforts of most of the smaller egg predators, although there is always the risk that the whole brood could be lost at once.

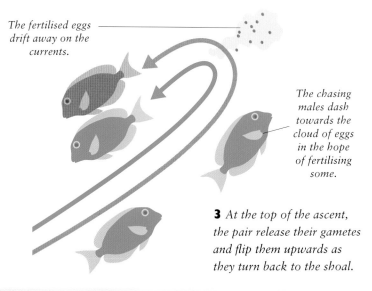

The fertilised eggs drift away on the currents.

The chasing males dash towards the cloud of eggs in the hope of fertilising some.

3 *At the top of the ascent, the pair release their gametes and flip them upwards as they turn back to the shoal.*

Getting it together

Around 80% of tropical marine fish broadcast their eggs and provide no parental care. Most of these such as angelfish, butterflyfish and surgeonfish, spawn in the hour around dusk. This is thought to give the eggs the greatest chance of survival, because fewer planktivores are actively feeding at dusk and water currents can carry the buoyant eggs away to safety under cover of darkness. Some fish species gather in pairs for their spawning ascent, but for others the situation seems more confusing as they gather into huge spawning aggregations.

Q: Do broadcast-spawning fish spawn in pairs or in groups?

A: Larger species of angelfish, such as the queen angelfish and the blue angelfish, which range over the reef feeding on dispersed food resources, are typically found in pairs, the female producing tens of thousands of eggs each evening. Other species, particularly those such as mandarinfish that live in territories, have a harem as

the breeding unit and males spawn with each of the females sequentially. Perhaps the most dramatic spawning events are those of fish such as grunts and blue tangs, which may migrate in their thousands to spawning sites in the late afternoon. However, the evidence seems to suggest that the spawning gathering is not simply a free-for-all. Males often defend their own area of the water column from other

males, while females can assess the males and approach to spawn, whereupon the pair will rise in their spawning ascent, sometimes with unwelcome male hangers-on. Other fish that form spawning aggregations, such as Nassau groupers, spawn

Below: At dusk, Synchiropus splendidus *begin to court. The larger male spreads his fins and the pair rise, releasing sperm and eggs.*

Left: Rock beauty angelfish (Holacanthus tricolor) *form long-lasting pair bonds. The female can release as many as 50,000 eggs.*

explosively, each individual spawning intensively for a relatively short period of time.

Q: Does this vary between populations?

A: The reproductive patterns of fish are not necessarily fixed; instead, the fish respond to the conditions in which they live. For example, cleaner wrasse usually live in harems of up to ten females with one male, but in some populations they switch to a simple male and female pair arrangement. Similarly, male blue-headed wrasses are highly territorial on small reefs with low wrasse populations, but on larger reefs, where the competition for space is so much more intense, males cannot defend against all other males so group-spawning becomes the norm.

Q: Where do the fish spawn?

A: The size of fish dictates to a large extent where they spawn. For smaller fish, such as gobies and some wrasse, travelling far from their home range to an ideal spawning site would expose them to all manner of patrolling predators. For this reason they tend to spawn near their own territories, making shorter spawning ascents than do larger broadcast-spawners. There are relatively few places on a reef that offer the optimum conditions for the survival and dispersal of eggs, such as strong currents and low predator densities. Therefore, larger fish are very often prepared to migrate to places with more preferential conditions in order to spawn.

Staying home for the kids

Broadcast spawning is not for everyone. Quite a few species of reef fishes produce demersal eggs; in other words, they lay their eggs directly onto the substrate of the reef. In almost all cases, these demersal eggs are laid in clumps, which are then jealously guarded by one or both parents. When the eggs hatch, the larvae are supplied by egg sacs for the first few hours of their lives. These give their organs and senses more time to develop and allow the larvae to move to the plankton-rich surface waters off the reef, where they can continue to grow amidst a rich food supply.

Q: *Which reef fish guard demersal eggs?*

A: Small reef fishes are limited by the number of eggs they can produce. The simple rule is that the smaller the fish, the fewer eggs it can lay, and most egg-guarding reef fish are small – less than 10cm long. When fish are limited by the number of eggs they can produce, it can pay to safeguard their eggs' early development by guarding them.

Around 20% of reef fishes guard their young, including damselfish, dottybacks, grammas, gobies, blennies and even larger species, such as triggers and filefishes.

Below: The titan triggerfish (Balistoides viridescens) *prepares a nest, arranging stones to its liking. The nest is guarded aggressively and curious divers may be attacked.*

Left: Male damselfish make excellent parents, protecting their vulnerable eggs as these gradually develop, attached to the substrate in a scraped nest.

Q: Why do they provide parental care instead of broadcast spawning?

A: Looking after developing eggs can be a costly business. It ties the parent to a particular place and guarding a clutch can make the adult more conspicuous to predators and dangerously distract its attention. Against this, the act of guarding ensures that a far smaller proportion of eggs is lost to predators. According to some estimates, about a third of the eggs of broadcast spawners are lost to predators every 24 hours. If eggs are guarded by a parent, these losses are far lower. Demersal spawning also means that parental fish need not leave the safety of the reef – an important consideration for smaller fish – and the greater survival of eggs in these reef miniatures makes it worthwhile for the caring parent.

Q: Are demersal eggs and young different to those of the broadcast spawners?

Demersal-spawning fish produce fewer eggs than broadcast spawners, ranging from just a few hundred to over a thousand, if a number of females contribute. But although this may seem a considerable amount, it represents a fraction of the number produced by larger broadcast spawners. Demersal eggs tend to develop at a slower rate, too, and spawning very often takes place early in the day, giving the young a longer period in which to grow and become independent. The larger size of demersal eggs also helps; though fewer in number, they are better provisioned than broadcast eggs. Finally, demersal eggs are usually adhesive, which allows them to stick to the substrate or, in the case of dottybacks, to hold together in a ball of eggs.

Q: What happens to the young when they hatch?

A: In most cases, the newly hatched young of demersal-spawning species join the fry of broadcast spawners in the plankton once they have absorbed their yolk sac, but there are exceptions. For example, newly hatched toadfishes remain close to the substrate throughout their development. However, this is a rare strategy because of the competition for space and the high predation risk on the reef.

Eggsitting

The fish that guard their progeny through the most vulnerable stages of their life expose themselves to risks and to costs that their egg-scattering cousins avoid completely. The reward for their diligence is the greater survival of their young. Eggsitting is most common amongst fish that live in close association with the surface of the reef, such as blennies and gobies, which hide their eggs away inside burrows or fissures. However, male damselfish tend their young in the open, exposing themselves to enormous risk.

Above: This male goby is guarding his brood, which has been laid on the side of a living sea squirt. Gobies usually lay eggs demersally.

Q: *Where is the safest place from which to guard the young?*

A: Demersal-spawning fish usually combine their feeding and breeding territories, so their food supply is never far from their precious eggs. This allows them to maintain their strength and their vital local knowledge of bolt-holes and refuges. The territories of blennies and gobies are usually well sheltered from excessive currents and from many predators. When the time

comes to spawn, the eggs can also be safely hidden away. In many of these species, females place great importance on the quality and location of the nest when deciding where to spawn. However, for herbivorous fish, such as damsels, territories need direct sunlight to encourage the growth of algae. This means that egg clutches are often fairly exposed and parents have to be extremely energetic in fending off the attentions of a host of different predatory threats.

Q: *Which parent does the guarding?*

A: In most cases, the male carries out the guarding duties. One reason for this is that, in guarding species, males are usually larger and thus better equipped to defend. Females are limited by the number of eggs they can produce and must feed extensively to replace lost reserves following spawning. By contrast, males can mate repeatedly and in many guarding species this is exactly what they do, filling their nests with the eggs of as many females as possible. In some species, the females do not take too kindly to this! Male ambon damselfish (*Pomacentrus amboinensis*) hold territories and breed with several different local females. Amongst these females, there is a dominant individual – a so-called primary female – who remains near the nest and determines which other females are allowed access and how many eggs they may lay. The bluebanded goby (*Valenciennea strigata*) lives its short life in a monogamous arrangement. The male guards the eggs while the female stays on the territory to make sure no interlopers turn up.

Q: *Do any demersal spawners care for their young beyond hatching?*

A: Given the number of freshwater fishes that look after both eggs and young, it may seem surprising that reef fish, by and large, provide little or no care for their newly hatched fry. Remember, however, that nearly all egg-guarding reef fish are small and would find it difficult to fight off the attentions of a myriad of predators of all sizes if they tried to defend a swarm of young, rather than

a much easier tight clump of stationary eggs. Nonetheless, there are some species that provide extended childcare. In much the same manner as some cichlids, spiny chromis (*Acanthochromis polyacanthus*) guard their young until they reach a few centimetres in length and apparently even feed them on the mucus of their flanks.

Below: Few fish live in such devotedly monogamous pairs as the bluebanded goby (Valenciennea strigata). *Both parents protect their eggs and territory.*

Guarding in pairs and groups

Although many adult reef fishes live territorially, this does not necessarily mean they must live alone. There are many instances of fish, such as wrasse, living in harems inside a territory with a single dominant male and a coterie of females. But these arrangements do not represent colonial arrangements; the male spawns separately with each female and the group as a whole does not usually defend the nest site. Picasso triggerfish live in a similar kind of arrangement in the wild; a single male defends a long-term territory containing two or three females and spawns with each in succession. Each female then takes care of the eggs without assistance from the male. If she fails to tend the nest, the male will not intervene and the clutch will rapidly be eaten. In other related species, such as the long-nosed filefish, both members of a pair contribute to territory and nest defence.

Right: Male Picasso triggerfish dominate large territories, while females tend to care for the eggs.

Q: *In some species both parents guard the eggs, but not in others. Why is this?*

A: When fish live in male/female pairs, each contributing to the defence of the nest, it is a matter of necessity rather than a cosy arrangement. In these cases, a single parent may not be able to defend a clutch effectively on its own and needs the back-up provided by their partner. Living in this manner seriously constrains the male's attempts to breed with as many females as possible. Recognising this, females of monogamous species tend to be highly aggressive towards other females. But even when only one parent normally does the guarding, the other parent may sometimes intervene in an emergency. Experiments in some goby species, where the male usually cares for the eggs on his own, have shown that if he is removed, the female will sometimes step in to guard her own eggs.

Q: *How about clownfish – don't they guard as a group?*

A: Most clownfish live in small groups, defending their home anemone. The group usually consists of a large dominant

Left: Pairs of long-nosed filefish work as a team to defend their patch. Their unusual and highly specific diet of certain kinds of coral probably contributes to this living arrangement.

Q: So are there any reef fish that nest colonially?

A: Certainly there are very few – but some do. Male green damselfish (*Abudefduf abdominalis*) live in colonial nesting groups and are thus better able to defend their nests communally from egg predators. Because of this, females prefer males in larger groups, knowing that picking a male from a large colony is likely to result in more of her eggs surviving. But this is not the end of the story for the males in the group. Even after a female has picked a male the others try to sneak in on the spawning act.

female and a breeding male, together with a small number of unrelated, non-breeding fish. But repeated experiments have failed to show that the breeding pair gain any direct benefit from the presence of their lodgers. The non-breeders certainly take no part in guarding the eggs or fanning or cleaning them. Instead, only the breeding pair cares for the eggs, and the bulk of the work is undertaken by the male, allowing the female to devote her time to replenishing her energy for the next spawning cycle. This has led researchers to wonder why, in this case, the breeding pair tolerate the presence of the others. There is some suggestion that although they provide no benefit, neither do the lodgers impose any costs. In addition, there are some reports that if

the breeding male is lost while there are eggs, the next male that steps up to the rank of breeder is bullied by the female into helping her care for the lost male's eggs.

Sharing the workload?

Clownfish live in small groups with a strict social hierarchy, but this does not necessarily mean that lower-ranked fish do most of the hard work.

1 *The dominant male fathers the offspring, but must tend the eggs without help from the other males.*

2 *If the male goes missing, the dominant female may coerce other group males to care for the eggs.*

Mouthbrooding in fish

No matter how good the spot in which parental fish choose to hide their eggs and young, a certain proportion of the brood – and sometimes all of it – will be lost to predators. One solution adopted by fish is to carry the young with them and this usually means in their mouths. The risk of being eaten on the reef relates to a fish's size – the smaller the fish, the greater the danger it faces. By carrying their eggs and/or young in their mouth, parental fish cut out a huge number of predators. To eat the young, a predator must also eat the parent.

Q: *Which reef fish use mouthbrooding?*

A: Although not as common in marine fishes as it is among their freshwater cousins, a few groups of fish do brood their young in this way, including cardinalfishes, sea catfish and jawfishes. Over the years, there have been claims of mouthbrooding behaviour in basslets but little evidence has been accumulated to back this up. One reason for the comparative rarity of this strategy amongst reef fish is that mouthbrooders are extremely limited by the number of eggs they can produce – no more,

obviously, than will fit in the mouth. Producing small numbers of young in a habitat so full of predators is clearly risky. That said, there are claims of brooding cardinalfish managing to accommodate several thousand eggs in their mouth at once.

Q: *Which parent does the brooding?*

A: Although mouthbrooding fishes seem to live in long-standing pair arrangements, it is always the male that cares for the young. After a typically energetic courtship, female cardinalfish produce a ball of eggs, which

Left: The newly released young of some mouthbrooding species, such as the Banggai cardinalfish (Pterapogon kauderni), *are perfect miniature replicas of their parents and well equipped to begin an independent life.*

the male fertilises before taking them into his mouth for safe-keeping for between one and two weeks. During this time, the male conscientiously keeps the eggs clean and aerates them by repeatedly spitting out and regathering the egg mass in his mouth. While he is brooding, the male must contend with two major problems: first of all, he is severely restricted in feeding and secondly, his own breathing is impaired. In the first case, the condition of parental males deteriorates over the breeding season to the point where, in desperate circumstances, the male is sometimes known to eat some of his brood. The second problem is solved to a large part by the amazing ability of mouthbrooding species to tolerate low oxygen intake.

Q: What happens to the young after they hatch?

A: In most species, the newly hatched young are released from their parent's mouth to undergo a pelagic larval stage of development, as occurs with most reef fishes. However, Banggai cardinalfish miss out this pelagic stage and continue to brood their offspring after hatching. To do this, the fry need a food supply in the shape of a yolk sac, which means that the

Above: A male tiger cardinalfish (Cheilodipterus macrodon) *brooding eggs in his mouth. The mass of eggs distends his mouth and throat, making it difficult to eat or even to breathe properly.*

eggs are larger to accommodate these extra supplies. The number of eggs that the male can brood is thus even more limited than in other species, and each brood represents a considerable investment for the parents. Newly released juvenile Banggai cardinalfish settle straight onto the reef, seeking shelter wherever they can find it, in crevices of the reef or even amongst the spines of sea urchins.

Livebearing in reef fish

Broadcasting huge numbers of eggs straight into the environment or preparing and defending a nest are both strategies that work well for the majority of fish. Some produce hundreds – even thousands – of eggs to try to guarantee that one or two might survive; others lay fewer eggs but protect them aggressively from danger. But some reef fishes invest even more heavily in their young, protecting them by brooding them internally.

Q: Which fish look after their young in this way?

A: A range of species brood their young, and they use different styles of brooding. Ghost pipefish (Solenostomidae) and seahorses and pipefish (Syngnathidae) have a special brood pouch in which keep the eggs. The difference between the two groups is that in ghost pipefish the female cares for the eggs, whereas in seahorses it is the male. Other families of reef fish brood their young internally, including some sharks and the extremely unusual-looking livebearing brotulas. These latter

exhibit internal fertilisation and the young hatch inside the female's body before birth.

Q: How do ghost pipefish brood their young?

A: In ghost pipefish, the female carries her eggs in a specialised pouch formed by her pair of modified pelvic fins. Inside this pouch, the eggs are attached to specialised cells called cotylephores. It is thought that these blood-rich cells may help in gas exchange for the brood, but whether or not this is the case, the female also pumps water into the pouch to oxygenate the eggs and to carry away waste products. The brood develops inside her pouch for two or three weeks before she carries them to a safe place, where she can release them a few at a time by rhythmically pulsing her pouch.

Q: How is this process different in seahorses?

A: One of the main differences is that female seahorses must insert their eggs into the male's brood pouch using an ovipositor. Fertilisation of the eggs happens once the eggs are inside the

pouch itself. This pouch, or marsupium, is a remarkable structure that protects the developing eggs and young and provides them with nutrients and oxygen. The male even secretes his own anti-bacterial proteins to keep any infections at bay. The male holds the brood (and sometimes additional broods) for up to approximately three weeks. During this time he provides a steady supply of liquid food directly from his body into the pouch. The extent to which the young are fed by their father varies between species. In

Above: A baby seahorse leaves the pouch. It has a greater chance of reaching adulthood than many other newly hatched reef fishes.

some species the eggs are well supplied by their mother, so the male does comparatively little to feed his offspring while they develop in his pouch. Females sometimes even provide a 'packed lunch' for their young, laying a few so-called nurse eggs whose function is to act as food reserves for the young inside the pouch. Other species of seahorse mothers are far less conscientious and lay much more basic, unprovisioned eggs. The job of supplying the developing offspring with food then falls predominantly to the male. In either case, when the food runs out it is time for the young to leave the safety of the pouch. The male releases his brood using muscular contractions of his body, propelling his progeny into the safest place he can find.

*Below: An incubating male lined seahorse (*Hippocampus erectus*). The eggs and young within the pouch, or marsupium, are supplied with oxygen, food and disinfectant!*

General index

Page numbers in **bold** indicate major entries; *italics* refer to captions and annotations; plain type indicates other text entries.

A

Aggression 14, 132, 135, 139, *140*, 142, 144, 146, 147, 153, 155, 161, 164, 166, 174, 194
in invertebrates **150-151**
in the aquarium 17, 149
Algae sp. 11, 12, 38, 74, 75, 76
as food 38, 44, 46, *46*, *62*, 63, 69, 71, 72, 73, 137, 140, *140*, 141, 192
symbiotic 9, 72, *72*, *73*, 75, 87, 151
Algal garden 137, 139, 153
Algal turf 67, 73, *74*, 75, 135
Anisogamy 160
Aposematism 108
Aquarist 69, 132, 149, 156
Aristotle's lantern *74*
Attack dilution 125

B

Bacteria 63, 73, 75
Behaviour 28, 30, 33, 34, 35, 38, 40, 42, *51*, 53, 54, 55, 129, 160, 170, 172
communicating through **16-17**
patterns 35, *53*, 161, 167

Benthic 61
Biological clock 42, 53
Body language 16
Boundary disputes 141
Breeding **160-179, 180-199**
condition 55
ground 140
groups 143
seasons 54-55, 167, 173
Broadcast (scatter)
spawning in corals 183
in fish 50, 58, 59, **186-187**, 188, 189, 191
Brooding, in corals 183
in fish 198

C

Camouflage 94, 95, **96-99**
Caribbean 9, 50, 55, *55*
Chemical cues 120
Chemical defences 84, 104, 105, 107, 108, 117
Chemical messages 20-21
Chemical signals 57
Chemical weapons **104-109**
Chemoreceptor cells 20, 24
Chemosensory cells 21, 90
Chemotaxis 21
Chromatophores 15
Cladocerans 88
Colonial nesting groups 195
Colour 12, 14, 97, 130, 144, *145*, 161, 165, 174, 175, *175*
as a warning 105, **108-109,** 152

changing *15*, *19*, 96
communicating through **14-15, 18-19**
coral 72
Colour pattern 14, 19, 41, *41*, *51*, 62, 64, 97, *97*, 100, 101, 108, 109, 125, 147, 155, 170, 172, 176
Commensalism 152
Communication, through behaviour **16-17**
through colour **14-15, 18-19**
through smell **22-23**
Competition 34, 63, 66, 68, 126, 134, 136, *137*, 138, 142, 144, 150, 162, 170, 173
Confusion effect **124-125**
Conspecific 35, 38, 61, 120, 124, 127, *130*, 131, 135, 142, 149
Contour elimination 98, 99
Cooperation 132, 133, **152-155**
Copepods 67, 70, 88
Coral reef **8-27**
as food **76-79,** 104
at night **48-51**
barrier 10
communities 11, 64, *66*, 77, 79, 92
diversity *10*, 79, 151
during the day **44-47**
ecology **10-11**
fore reef 11
fringing *10*, 11
hiding places 102, 103
life cycle *45*, 49, 56
platform *10*

spur and groove zones 134
year round **54-55**
Cotylephore 198
Counter-shading 96
Courtship 14, 17, 23, 27, 172, 173, *173*, 174, 175, *175*, 176, 177, 178

D

Day length 42, 44, 54, 55
Demersal spawning 45, 50, 58, 59, *59*, **190-191**, 192, 193
Displays 132, 133, 142, 146, 147, 148, 172, 173, **174-175**, 176, 178
Dominance heirarchies 128, **142-143**, 153, 166
in corals 151
Dominance status 171
Drumming 26

E

Egg 23, 25, 42, 44, 45, 46, 50, 52, 54, 57, **58-59**, 60, 61, 62, 64, 65, 70, 104, 137, 138, 141, 144, 160, 163, 166, *167*, *169*, 170, 172, 173, 176, 177, 179, *179*, **180-199**
nurse 199
sitting **192-193**
demersal 180
guarding 180, **190-195**
Embryo 23, *23*, 45, 58, 59, 60,

Index to fish and invertebrates

Credits

The publishers would like to thank the following photographers for providing images, credited here by page number and position: (B) Bottom, (T) Top, (C) Centre, (BL) Bottom left, etc.

Aqua Press: 189(T), 191, 194, 196, 199

Clay Bryce: 17(BL), 19(TR), 25, 42(TL), 47(BR), 48, 50, 51, 84, 97(B), 102, 105(T), 108, 116(T,B), 117(B), 124, 126, 157(BR), 158, 159, 176, 177, 180(C), 184

John Gionis: 56

Scott Michael: 22-23, 29, 39, 42(BC), 59(BR), 62, 66, 75, 76, 79, 80, 82, 83, 93(B), 95, 100(B), 101(T), 109(T,BR), 111, 114(TC), 120, 121(B), 130(both), 131, 132(BL), 133(TR,BL), 134, 135, 139, 148, 150, 152, 154(B), 156, 157(TL), 162, 163, 164, 174(C,B), 179, 185(T,B), 187, 192, 197

Alf Nilsen: 8, 9, 17(TR), 18, 28, 31, 33, 34, 43, 44, 45, 46, 47(T), 49, 52, 59(TL), 60, 63, 64, 68, 69, 74, 77, 85, 86(T,C),

87, 90-91, 94, 96, 97(T,C), 98, 99(BR), 103, 104, 105(BL), 118-119(B), 125, 127, 129, 142, 146-147, 151(T,B), 153, 155, 161, 169(BL,BR), 178, 182, 190

Photomax: 188, 198

J E Randall: 65

Graeme Robinson: 54

Geoff Rogers © Interpet Publishing Ltd: 8(TL), 12, 13(TL,TR,BR), 14(C,BR), 15(C,B), 16, 24, 26, 27, 28(TL), 30(C,BL), 36, 40, 53, 58, 66(TL), 70, 72, 78(BL), 78-79(T), 81, 88-89, 92, 93(T), 94(TL), 99(T), 100(C), 101(B), 106(BL), 106-107(T), 107(B), 109(BC), 110, 113, 114(BL), 115, 118(TL), 123, 132(TL), 144-145(T), 145(TR), 154(TR), 160(TL), 168, 169(T), 170, 171(T,C,B), 172-173, 180(TL), 193

Rudolf Svensen UWPhoto: 181

Iggy Tavares: 35, 38, 167, 195

Illustration references

The computer graphics on the pages shown have been based on the following sources:

Page 10 : *The Modern Coral Reef Aquarium Volume 1* by Svein A Fossa and Alf Jacob Nilsen, Birgit Schmettkamp Verlag, Bornheim (1996)

Page 11 : *The Modern Coral Reef Aquarium Volume 1* by Svein A Fossa and Alf Jacob Nilsen, Birgit Schmettkamp Verlag, Bornheim (1996)

Page 15 : *Fish and Their Behavior* by G K H Zupanc 2nd edition, Tetra-Press, Melle (1988)

Page 68: *The Ecology of Fishes on Coral Reefs* by Peter F. Sale. Academic Press Inc.

Page 71: *The Ecology of Fishes on Coral Reefs* by Peter F. Sale. Academic Press Inc.

Page 74: *Invertebrate Zoology* by Robert D Barnes, Holt-Saunders (1980) After Cuenot.

Page 84 *Invertebrate Zoology* by Robert D Barnes, Holt-Saunders (1980) Modified after Clench.

Author's acknowledgements

Thanks to my wonderful wife, Alison, for her help with this book. Thanks to my parents, Barbara and Gerald, for everything. Finally, thanks also to Professor Jens Krause, whose patience and guidance have been invaluable.

Publisher's acknowledgements

The publishers would like to thank the following for their help in providing facilities for photography: Amwell Aquatics, Soham, Cambridgeshire. Cheshire Water Life, Sandiway, Cheshire. Interfish, Wakefield, Yorkshire. Maidenhead Aquatics, Crowland, Lincolnshire. Tuan Pham. Sevenoaks Tropical Marine, Sevenoaks, Kent. Shirley Aquatics, Solihull, Warwickshire. Swallow Aquatics, Aldham, Colchester, Essex. Swallow Aquatics, East Harling, Norfolk. Swallow Aquatics, Rayleigh, Essex. Swallow Aquatics, Southfleet, Kent. Tropical Marine Centre, Chorleywood, Hertfordshire. Tropical Marine Centre, Wythenshawe, Manchester. Wharf Aquatics, Pinxton, Nottinghamshire.

Publisher's note